DICK SUTPHEN'S

WISDOM

DICK SUTPHEN'S

WISDOM

ROBERTA SUTPHEN

MEDIA

Published 2023 by Gildan Media LLC
aka G&D Media
www.GandDmedia.com

Front cover design by David Rheinhardt of Pyrographx

Designed by Meghan Day Healey of Story Horse, LLC.

Library of Congress Cataloging-in-Publication Data is available upon request

ISBN: 978-1-7225-0658-2

10 9 8 7 6 5 4 3 2 1

Contents

Part 1
BASIC PRINCIPLES

Part 2
PRACTICAL APPLICATIONS

Part 3
ISSUES IN HYPNOSIS

Part 4
THE MULTIMILLIONAIRE MINDSET

Part 5
COLUMNS, 1979–2004

Contents

Preface

Known to the world as Dick Sutphen, Richard Charles Sutphen was the love of my life, or as he always said, "the love of my lives." We were together in so many lifetimes that it was hard to trace them all. We had that instant connection he taught was possible in his Soulmate Seminars.

My lifetime with Dick was not about being together but about a mission we both shared. His mission was to bring in his knowledge of hypnosis and metaphysics, and I was to make sure it was held in the Light and brought out for generations to come.

Each day I feel the pain of this loss, yet he is still with me, just in another form. Whenever I become overwhelmed with grief, he reminds me of our shared agreement. It took me almost two years before I could put this book together without crying, yet I've always known of my dharmic duty to God, to my husband, and to society. Even though he's left the physical world, I still feel married to him, for he continues to give me his love and advice from the spirit world.

Richard played an important role in the making of this book. At times I would wake up knowing I had to find a certain lecture or script to include, or when he would insist that I include his Subpersonalities Process, which I had not planned to do. He even helped me with this preface. It was going to be a typical introduction until he pointed out how to avoid a boring, chronological retelling of events. I have his ten three-ring binders of notes, which he would point to whenever I wanted him to teach me his skills. It felt too much like homework, and so I confess I have only read through one of those binders.

By 2010, I had jumped off my last yachting position and jumped into my life with Richard and Sutphen Seminars. I'd studied metaphysics through meditative communications with my Spirit Guide since I was a child, but I'd never worked in the "industry." Richard made the transition easy for me, and soon I was accompanying him to seminars and helping him with his private sessions. We worked so well together.

Richard had some personal issues, which resulted in his losing quite a bit of his life's work, and I tried my best to help him by retyping all the material you see in this book. During the many years we shared, we loved, lived, and worked together, and I ended up knowing his material inside and out.

No one is perfect, yet Richard was perfect in my eyes. He had learned all the lessons life threw at him and rose above the noise every time. He was calm, cool, and collected and responded with patience and kindness to every situation. He was the only truly self-actualized person I have known who had freedom from the self.

When Dick had his last stroke at Christmas 2019, I expected him to make another full recovery; however, Covid-19 soon hit. We were unable to receive the care he needed, and I watched my husband quickly fade away. He never complained! Not once. He was more concerned about me and what I was going through. I'm not exaggerating when I say the room filled with light as he passed into Spirit. I knew he was right beside me as the health workers came by, because I could feel his arm around my shoulder. At his request and insistence, I had a private funeral for him and buried him next to his mother and father in the Sutphen family plot in Omaha, Nebraska.

We didn't have much time together, but we knew what we had to do. I wasn't expecting him to die at the age of eighty-three. I truly thought we had another ten years when we could actually retire and enjoy life again. That didn't happen. It has taken all my belief in God and my knowledge of metaphysics to get through this time without him.

Even though he and I still talk every day, and even though we can hug in the ethers or in my mental eye, it's not physical, and I miss him like crazy. Dick Sutphen was a gift to the world, to me and to his family. What a special man!

The material in this book is taken from a collection of his papers and talks spanning the decades. They have been edited to a certain extent for the sake of consistency and organization and to avoid unnecessary repetitions.

Roberta Sutphen
March 2022

Part 1
BASIC PRINCIPLES

The writings in this section set out the main principles of Dick's metaphysical worldview. It's valuable to be familiar with them in order to understand the reasoning and methods behind his therapeutic process.

How Your Mind Works

There are three levels of mind: the conscious, the subconscious, and the superconscious; the last is also called Higher Self.

1. The conscious mind: will, reason, logic, and the five physical senses.

2. The subconscious mind: the memory banks containing all your past programming, including beliefs, habit patterns, emotional programming, and the Akashic (astral) records of all the lifetimes you have ever lived.

3. The superconscious mind (Higher Self): the creative force and psychic abilities, the collective awareness of mankind, plus unlimited but unknown powers.

The Higher Self

When you attain a Higher Self level of consciousness, you have at your mental fingertips an awareness of your totality and the collective totality of the energy gestalt we can call *God*. We are all part of the collective unconscious—the greater body of mankind—thus we are all one.

In my book *You Were Born Again to Be Together*, I wrote about Higher Self:

The superconscious mind is often referred to meta-physically as the Higher Self—the God self or the I AM. It is the power behind creative and psychic abilities. It is also unlimited in power and wisdom. Every man has consummate genius within him. By opening the doors to the superconscious, you can do anything as long as you use the power in a positive way. Thus you have the ability to self-bestow your own happiness and success, or to achieve help and guidance beyond anything we can consciously imagine.

Within this Higher Self level there is a larger, universal perspective of which we must be aware when seeking the truth. We judge from an earthbound perspective, based on logic, sequential time, and science. Earthbound perspective would claim heredity and environment determine our lives. Universal perspective would teach that you choose your parents, environment, and time and place of birth for the experience and opportunities they offer, and that your present-life circumstances were determined by your past lives and your programming in your current incarnation.

If we could truly know ourselves—our Higher Selves—we would live in a world of cooperation, love, and wisdom.

The Subconscious and the Conditioned Mind

A man kept a goose in a bottle, feeding it until it grew too large to get through the bottleneck. How can he get the goose out of the bottle without killing it or destroying the bottle?

This Zen koan offers a choice between two alternatives, both of which are equally impossible. The koan reflects the dilemma of life: the problem of passing beyond the two alternatives of assertion and denial, both of which obscure the truth. The real problem is not to get the goose out of the bottle, but rather to get ourselves out. The goose represents man and the bottle, his circumstances. Our bottleneck is our conditioned way of seeing things. We see situations and problems as alien objects standing in our way rather than as extensions of our own consciousness. We are conditioned to believe that our mind is inside us and that our perceptions of the world are outside. In reality, our mind is outside and all that we perceive is within our mind. Or, to put it another way, "The goose is out!"

Every thought you've ever had, every word you've ever spoken, and every action you've ever experienced is recorded in the memory banks of your subconscious mind. This also includes all the memories of previous lifetimes.

According to brain researchers, the subconscious mind has 200,000 times the capacity of the largest computer ever built, so recording the history of your lives really isn't too great a task. Since the human mind works like a computer in certain respects, all your past experiences represent your software programming, which has made you what you are today. Your talents and abilities, your problems and afflictions, are the result of this subconscious programming. Your subconscious has directed you, and it will continue to direct you. Sadly, it is often in opposition to your conscious desires.

The subconscious creates only according to its programming. It will bring into actuality the reality for which it is programmed. This may have nothing to do with what you consciously desire, relating only to the past programming (thoughts and experiences) it has received.

For example: You'd like to be able to go boating with your friends, but for some reason, you experience a great deal of anxiety whenever you get into a boat. Consciously, you realize there is minimal danger in boating, yet the anxiety persists.

Why? Because the subconscious has no reasoning power. It simply operates like a computer. It functions as the result of programming. Maybe you experienced a fearful, though forgotten, trauma involving water as a child, or maybe you drowned in a past life. The result was negative programming, and although the past experience may not relate to the present, you still experience the anxiety.

If the subconscious were to receive no new programming, it would continue to operate on past input. This, of course, cannot happen, for you are constantly feeding new programming or data into your computer: your subconscious mind. Every thought programs the computer. If your thoughts are more negative than positive, your computer is being programmed negatively.

Your subconscious mind is a memory bank of everything you've ever thought, said, or done. Your subconscious mind holds the memory of what your mother's doctor said at your birth, what you did on your fourth birthday, and who you had dinner with ten years ago.

The most important fact about the subconscious is that it can be fooled. It is like a computer that doesn't know where the information is coming from; it only knows to act on it. Hypnosis brings you into an altered state where you can easily reprogram your mind. You have the power to change your life!

Altered States

Hypnosis and meditation are both altered states of consciousness. When your mind is in an altered state, you are 25 to 200 times as suggestible, which is why hypnosis can be so powerful. Being in an altered state does not mean you are "tranced out" but rather that you are in a relaxed state and are focused upon one thing.

Being in an altered state is not unnatural. You experience this state two-thirds of the time while you are watching TV. Runners go into an altered state as they hit their rhythm and natural pace. Writers go into an altered state if they are focused upon what they are writing, losing track of time. Those who work at repetitive jobs, such as on assembly lines, go into an altered state. Any time you are totally absorbed in what you are doing, you are in an altered state of mind.

Some call this being in the "flow." So being in the flow is being in an altered state of mind. This has nothing to do with training or education. It happens to us all.

Visualization is the ultimate programming technique. This is where you tell your mind what is going to happen. You see it as a real experience, including how it feels to have it already accomplished. Visualization tells your mind that this is going to happen; therefore your mind creates it as a reality.

Visualization is an extremely powerful tool and numerous studies have been done to test it. In one famous study conducted at the University of Chicago, subjects were basketballs players who were split into three groups. Each group was tested on how many free throws they could make. The first group practiced free throws every day for an hour. The second group merely visualized themselves making free throws. The third group did nothing.

After thirty days, the subjects were tested again. The first group improved by 24 percent. The second group improved by 23 percent—without touching a basketball. The third group, as expected, did not improve.

You *Are* Mind

You create your own reality, or karma, with your thoughts. Many people have no idea how frequently they think in a negative manner. If you climb out of bed cursing the alarm clock, grumble your way through breakfast, dwell on how much you dislike the rain and traffic during your commute to work, brood unhappily about your job, and go on and on in this fashion throughout the day, you are creating a worse reality for yourself. Because you are thinking more negative thoughts than positive ones, there is simply no way you can be creating anything but a negative reality. With all that negative programming, how can your computer do anything but create the programmed result: more negativity?

You do not *have* a mind, you *are* mind. You are using your current body, but your body isn't you. You have a soul or a spirit. It must be mind, because regressive hypnosis will show that it carries all the memories of the past. Every individual carries memories of previous lifetimes, and the events in these past lives often seem to be affecting the present. This in itself does not prove the fact of reincarnation, but does show that a lineage of cause and effect—karma—is evident.

If you are a mind and that mind operates like a computer, that makes you a computer—a machine. Naturally, there is more to you than this mechanical aspect, but few people are presently working with larger aspects of their totality.

Everyone has the potential to create their own reality. What mind has created, mind can change. The subconscious mind doesn't reason, but it does appear to generate circumstances that create a reality reflecting the programming it receives. This is normally accomplished by thoughts and through life experiences. But brain researchers have found that the subconscious is incapable of telling the difference between reality and fantasy—between the real experience and the imagined experience.

Karma and Reincarnation

I contend that either this is a random universe or there is some kind of plan. By "random universe," I mean that we evolved over the centuries to our present state, and when we die, we become nothing. If this is so, life is meaningless. But if there is a plan, then it would follow that there is an intelligence behind the plan. You can call this intelligence George, Ginger, God, Universal Mind, an energy gestalt, the collective unconscious, or any other name that works for you.

If there is a plan, wouldn't it also follow that justice would be part of the plan? But look around you. Where is the justification for all the misery and inequality in the world? How can you justify child abuse, mass starvation, rapes, murders, wars, victims of violence, people ripping off others and seemingly being rewarded for it?

Karma can explain it all. I've studied philosophy and religion all my adult life, and nothing else can logically explain the inequality. Karma rewards and punishes. It is a multilife debit and credit system, which offers total justice.

Karma either is or it isn't. There can be no halfway plan, no halfway justice. Either absolutely everything is karmic or nothing is karmic. You need to accept or reject the concept of karma; it is senseless and confusing to accept a halfway position.

To illustrate this process, if I pick up a stone and toss it into a pond, I am the cause, and the effect is the splash and ripples. I have disturbed the harmony of the pond. The ripples flow out and back until, by the physical law of dissipation of energy, the pond eventually returns to its original harmonious state.

Like the stone, your thoughts, words, and actions create vibrations that flow out into the universe and back to you until eventually, over many lifetimes, you balance your karma, and your harmony is restored.

Everything you think, say, and do creates or erases karma. And as if that's not enough to deal with, this includes the motive, intent, and desire behind every thought, word and action. That being the case, every aspect of life relates to spirituality. *Life is spirituality. Life itself is the spiritual quest, even if you do not meditate or pray or think positive.*

Maybe your life is about struggling to make a living at the gas station, and you enjoy bowling and drinking beer in the bar with your buddies. Still, you're here on earth on your spiritual quest.

Sure, meditating is spiritual. Attempting to be more positive is spiritual. But so is sex. So is vacuuming the carpet. So is taking the family dog to the vet. Life is spirituality. Labeling one thing as holy or spiritual while labeling another thing as something else is a mistake.

Your earthly purpose is to attain liberation *of* the self and *from* the self. Liberation from the self is a matter of rising above all fear-based emotions.

Let's look at some fear-based emotions:

Prejudice. Maybe you're prejudiced toward another race or another religion. Or maybe you're prejudiced against men, if you're a woman, or the other way around, or against homosexuals or bisexuals. If you're bi or gay, maybe you're prejudiced against straight people. Or maybe you're prejudiced against rich people.

Blame is another fear-based emotion that most of us can relate to. You blame one or both of your parents, or you blame an ex-husband, ex-wife, ex-lover, friend, business partner, or the careless driver that caused an accident that affected you.

Jealousy and possessiveness. Two more fear-based emotions that most of us can relate to. We usually don't have to look too far back into our past to find a situation in which we have displayed one or both of these qualities. Here are some more fear-based emotions:

Anger	Envy
Selfishness	Greed
Hate	Guilt
Repression	Egotism

And there are fears of avoidance:

Fear of intimacy	Fear of failure
Fear of commitment	Fear of success
Fear of responsibility	

Then you have to look at your obsessions, dependencies, and addictions. They too are fear-based emotions.

Your fear-based emotions are your karma—the reason that you have been reincarnated for another round on Mother Earth. But these fears are not real. They are old programming you came back to resolve. They're delusions.

When you begin to explore the motive, intent, and desire behind everything you think, say, and do, you'll find you're asking yourself a lot of questions. Are you helping your friend out of true compassion or because it pumps your ego? Or because your friend is now in debt to you? Do you give to charity at the office because you desire to help, or because you are afraid of what people in the office will think if you don't? It's easy to look as if you're creating harmonious karma when you really aren't, because your motive, intent, or desire are not what they appear to be. From a karmic perspective, *why* you do what you do is just as important as *what* you do.

I also contend that neither God nor the Lords of Karma bestow your suffering upon you. It is your decision and yours alone to either accept or refuse to deal with the opportunities you are experiencing in your life. You are responsible for absolutely everything that has ever happened to you. You are your own judge and jury. On a Higher Self level, you are aware that in order to progress, you must learn. And the fastest way to learn is by directly experiencing the consequences of your own actions.

If you and you alone are responsible for everything that has ever happened to you, that means there is no one to blame for anything that has ever happened to you. There is no one to blame for anything! The concept of blame is totally incompatible with karma.

There are no victims. The ex-mate you had such a hard time with, the partner who ripped you off, the in-laws you hated, your sadistic boss, the guy who raped you when you were twelve, the burglars who robbed your house—you created them all because you needed the balance and the test.

Take a moment and think back on your life. Think about everyone in your past who really made life difficult for you. In actuality, these were the people who helped you the most in accomplishing your goal of spiritual evolution. They helped you balance your karma. They were a test you created to determine how you're progressing.

It is easy to tell whether you are passing or failing your own tests. If you respond with love, positive thoughts, compassion, or even neutrality and can fully let go of the past, you are probably passing the test. If you respond with negativity, blame, or desire for revenge, you are probably failing the test.

If you choose to fail, that's all right; you'll just have to come back and try it again, probably with the same person. If one person learns and the other doesn't, the one who didn't learn will connect with someone who has similar karmic configurations, and they will come together to test themselves in the future.

Learning through Karma

Often in balancing karma, you don't even have to wait for the next lifetime for an opportunity to arise. We have all observed recurring undesirable patterns in others, as well as in ourselves. This is a situation of learning through pain until we finally "get it," once and for all, that what we are doing doesn't work.

You were born with a package of karma that you desired to experience. From a spiritual perspective, if you are testing yourself, it is only your reactions to the experiences that are important.

When we are on the other side in Spirit, preparing to enter into a lifetime, we seem to be very brave. For instance, you may say to yourself, "OK, I think I'm ready to test myself in another relationship with Donald. If he's willing, we'll fall in love, get married, and have three children. When I'm about thirty-two, Donald will begin to ignore me and start having affairs with other women. This time, because I owe Don one in this area, I'll emotionally support him and let him go with unconditional love."

Now comes the reality. What do you do? You scream and threaten and blame. You hire a lawyer, who socks it to Donald financially for the rest of his days. You and Donald now hate each other. This is another example of learning through pain. You and Don can plan to return for another round in the year 2046; maybe next time you'll work it out.

Actually, there is no such thing as failing your own karmic test. If you fell off your bicycle nine times before you finally learned to ride, the nine failures were actually small successes, which eventually led to the ultimate success. How many times you fail before reaching your goal is up to you.

In addition to your birth karma, you create new karma every day, both harmonious and disharmonious. And you pay it off every day through the balancing effects of your subconscious mind. There is also karma as yet unknown to you. It is stored up from the past, awaiting a suitable opportunity to discharge itself. This could happen later in this life, in your next life, or in the lifetime after that. Not everything can be balanced in one lifetime.

The good news is, the law of grace supersedes the law of karma. This means that if you give love, grace, and mercy, you will receive it in return. All of your positive, loving thoughts and actions go to cancel your stored-up bad karma. Since this is so, it is probably time for you to begin thinking how you can be more positive, loving, and compassionate and how you can support good works and serve this planet—if only to reduce the amount of undesirable karma that you have waiting for you in your future.

I also contend that wisdom erases karma and that we can mitigate karmic discomforts through awareness. The techniques of past-life therapy are often of value in this area. In the past, we've learned through pain. In other words, we've learned not to touch hot stoves because by touching hot stoves, we burn our fingers. After experiencing the pain of a few burnt fingers, we finally learn, once and for all, that this is a bad idea. Karmic lessons are the hot stoves we need to learn from in life.

To learn through wisdom, you must forgive yourself. Since you are your own judge and jury, it is up to you to forgive yourself. The only problem is that you will not do this unless on the level of Higher Mind you know the karma is totally balanced or that the lesson is learned. You can't fool yourself in this area. To truly forgive yourself, you must know, on every level of your body and mind, that you will never, ever forget the lesson again. Of course, to release the karma, you must also be able to sincerely forgive all the others involved.

Symbolic Restitution

If you are not yet able to forgive to this degree but you are determined to rise above the karmic effect, you must decide what you can do to achieve this desired level of self-forgiveness. Can you do something symbolic to show that you have learned? Can you assist others as a form of restitution?

Through working with people in past-life therapy, I've found that a technique I call "symbolic restitution" can be very helpful. As an example, a woman named Susan wanted but could not have a baby. She and her husband consulted doctors and subjected themselves to every kind of fertility test. In the end, the tests showed that there was no physical reason the woman could not conceive. "It must be a mental block," her doctor explained, suggesting she see a psychiatrist.

Instead, Susan explored a "back to the cause" hypnotic regression and reexperienced abandoning a baby in eighteenth-century England. Instead of making sure the child was cared for, the Englishwoman left it in the woods to die. In the Higher Self portion of the session, she was told, "You must learn the value of life, what a blessing it is to have a child, and about the responsibility of being a parent. Until you know these things, you will not trust yourself to birth another."

As a form of symbolic restitution, Susan became a volunteer in a Shriners hospital for crippled children. The last time I talked to her, she said, "I see the parents in agony over what their children are going through. I cry over the little ones when they return from the operating room. I have such a different perspective now."

I'll bet one day soon I'll receive a birth announcement from Susan.

The Five Kinds of Karma

Knowledge of past lives can help us to better understand that which influences, restricts, or motivates us in the present. Sometimes just knowing the cause of the problem resolves the effect.

After many decades of directing past-life regressions, I've found I can fit any kind of karma into one of five basic categories. Sometimes this situation will cover two of these categories at one time. As an example, balancing karma might also be reward karma. Physical karma might also be balancing karma.

Balancing Karma

This is the most simplistic, mechanical kind of cause and effect. Examples of balancing karma would be a lonely man who seeks unsuccessfully to establish a relationship. In a past life, he used others so cruelly that he needs to learn the value of a relationship. Other examples:

A man who is always overlooked for promotion because in a past life he destroyed others to attain wealth and power; a woman who suffers continual, severe migraine headaches because, in a fit of jealousy, she hit her lover on the head and killed him in a past life; a man who is born blind because as a Roman soldier, he purposely blinded Christian prisoners.

A man fearful of responsibility saw himself as a sea captain who abandoned his burning ship in the first lifeboat, leaving many of his crew to die.

An overly possessive husband observed a life in which the roles were reversed, and his mate (his wife in this life as well) ran away with a lover, leaving him alone to raise three children.

Physical Karma

Physical karma is a situation in which a past-life problem or misuse of the body results in an appropriate affliction in a later life. Physical karma often results from reincarnating too soon—before the etheric body has reformed.

As an example, a man with pneumonia had his lungs drained through a tube and was left with a deeply indented scar under his left arm. Upon dying, he remained on the other side only a short time before being reborn as a female with a blood sac under her left arm. Examining the baby, the doctor said, "There's a hole there. If it doesn't close on its own, we'll have to go in and sew it up."

Other examples: A child born with lung problems might have died from lung cancer due to excessive smoking in a past life. Another man had a disfiguring birthmark that was a carry-over from a terrible burn in another incarnation. A young woman with a birthmark on her arm regressed to 1938 and observed herself sitting before a fireplace. A large coal popped out and landed on her arm, causing a severe burn.

False-Fear Karma

False-fear karma is created when a traumatic past-life incident generates a fear that is not valid in the context of the current life.

For example, a workaholic discovered during regression that he was unable to feed his family during a time of famine in the Middle Ages. In his past-life regression, he reexperienced the pain of burying a child who starved to death. In his current life, his subconscious mind is attempting to avert any potential duplication of that terrible pain, thus generating an internal drive to work day and night to assure adequate provisions for his family in this incarnation.

Another instance of false-fear karma: A woman wanting to write New Age articles broke into a trembling sweat every time she tried. In regression she saw herself being burned at the stake for communicating similar ideas.

False-fear karma and false-guilt karma are the easiest to resolve through past-life therapy techniques, because once the individuals understand the origin of the fear and/ or guilt, they can see how it no longer applies to them in their current lifetime.

False-Guilt Karma

False-guilt karma occurs when an individual takes on the responsibility or accepts the blame for a traumatic past-life incident for which he or she is actually blameless.

A man who contracted polio resulting in a paralyzed leg perceived as the past-life cause his driving a car which was involved in an accident that crippled a child. Although it wasn't his fault, he blamed himself and sought self-forgiveness through this karmic affliction.

Continuing problems involving depression, pain, and/ or emotional trauma can usually be traced back to a past tragedy of some kind in which guilt is associated with the event. This can be false guilt or a situation in which the troubled individual was actually responsible for the tragedy.

Developed Ability and Awareness Karma
(Reward Karma)

Abilities and awareness are developed over a period of many lifetimes.

As examples: a man in Rome became interested in music and began to develop his ability in it. Today, after six additional lifetimes in which he refined his ability during each incarnation, he is a successful professional musician.

A woman happily married for thirty-five years has worked hard to refine her awareness of human relationships over many lifetimes.

In one regression, a woman art director saw herself serving as a male apprentice to a prominent portrait painter in Renaissance Italy.

The abilities and awareness that you master over a period of lifetimes are yours to keep forever, although they may lie latent, buried deep within you, waiting for a time when it is appropriate to call them into your present existence.

Why Are You Here?

Karma is the supreme Universal law. It is the basis of our reality. You know this, yet you haven't totally accepted it. Or maybe you don't understand its full implications. If you did, you would immediately change a few things about yourself.

A metaphysical axiom says, "Man always follows the highest path for which he is really certain." Most likely, you are following the highest path of which you are really certain . . . and the result is your current life, just the way it is.

The Seven Karmic Paths

If your life isn't the way you want it to be, suspend your beliefs for a few minutes and explore with an open mind the seven karmic paths:

No path. This path is best expressed in poet William Blake's words: "The road to excess leads to the palace of wisdom." Those on this path will eventually, through experience and pain, will perceive what has value and what doesn't. They judge everything from a perspective of self, and often they have difficulty determining what action will result in harmony as opposed to disharmony. These people appear to have little sense of balance and are usually unwilling to accept responsibility for their own lives.

Beginning path. These people are more responsible, but they enjoy having things handed to them. They want everything done "their way" and are materialistic and pleasure-oriented. Chances are, those on the beginning path will not have much interest in anything they can't eat, touch, or enjoy.

Intermediate path. Those on this path are beginning to realize that there is an alternate reality. They might become interested in spiritual matters, but tend to be drawn to dogmatic thinking. While they are less self-oriented than most, they usually remain materialistic and pleasure-centered.

Balanced path. Those on this path have an awareness of karma and carefully consider their actions, because they are aware of the ramifications. They are beginning to comprehend unconditional love and seek to detach from the standard illusions about reality. They begin to recognize that life can be experienced as a hostile separateness or a tranquil oneness. They don't repress their natural urges, but refrain from excess.

Harmonious path. These people require their outer lives to be in harmony with their inner beliefs. They live their spiritual philosophy. They are beginning to incorporate unconditional love and acceptance into their lives and have risen above blame and judgment. They accept *what is* and are well on the road to developing detached mind. Most of those on this path practice meditation in some form.

Force of will path. This path incorporates extreme discipline. It is the path of Zen monks, yoga devotees, and some priests, as well as many others who center their lives around spiritual faith. This may mean extreme dietary practices and celibacy. The argument for this path is that it is a rapid way to advance spiritually. The primary argument against it is that it is undesirable to drop out of the "real" world and repress your natural urges and desires, because if you do, they will increase in intensity. Even if you manifest the self-discipline to deal with them in this life, you may generate a karmic charge that you will have to deal with in a future life.

Bodhisattva path. Those on this path are beyond seeking. They are truly "in the world, but not of it." Only those who are highly evolved are capable of walking this path. They are living examples of detached mind and are dedicated to assisting others to find their way out of the darkness and into the spiritual light.

The Seven Dharmic Directions

Dharma is your duty to yourself and to society. This means following a course of action that is right for you. It will be something you do naturally and well. Following your dharmic or self nature will enable you to most easily raise your vibrational level of awareness. Through all your experiences, your karma conditions you to create the character required to carry out your dharma.

The best way to resolve your karma is to follow your dharmic direction: the direction that is natural and destined for you. There are seven general dharmic directions. It is your purpose to explore one of these paths with a particular soul goal that you chose prior to your birth.

Workforce involves the largest number of souls. This path encompasses most general occupations and homemakers.

Military includes soldiers, police and militia, and all those who enforce the laws of the country, state, and city.

Service includes most religious workers, those in medical, welfare and social services, many practicing metaphysicians, and those offering holistic health services.

Creativity includes artists, writers, poets, musicians, actors, dancers, and entertainers.

Science encompasses medical researchers, scientists, space technologists, and physicists.

Philosophy involves all who present theories about why man does what he does and how he might end suffering. Some church leaders would be included, along with philosophers and some metaphysical communicators.

Government includes political leaders, from the president of the United States to senators, governors, mayors, and anyone elected to office. It also includes those who take office by force through revolution.

The Seven Goals

In addition to having chosen one of seven karmic paths and seven dharmic directions prior to your birth, you have also chosen one of the seven basic soul goals. You may have more than one goal, but one will be most important; the next, secondary in importance; and so on.

Whether you consciously realize it or not, karmically you have definite life goal priorities. These goals all amount to karmic self-testing, with an overall goal of spiritual growth. Here are the seven goals:

Attain knowledge. Grasping a particular area of knowledge, which, when realized on a soul level, becomes wisdom. For example, the desire for awareness could include areas such as direct knowledge of humility, devotion, sacrifice, selflessness, or perseverance.

Open spiritually. This goal is to integrate spiritual awareness into your particular dharmic direction.

Achieve inner harmony. This goal amounts to attaining balance and peace of mind while fulfilling your particular dharmic duty.

Attain fame or power. Both elements of this goal are karmic rewards. They offer unique opportunities to test yourself, communicate awareness, and exert leadership.

Learn acceptance. This goal can be summarized as an awareness that what is, *is*, because resistance to *what is* causes suffering.

Provide support. This goal could range from the encouragement and support of another individual to helping accomplish a jointly shared dharmic direction or advancing an ideal or philosophical or religious belief.

Develop talents. Talents are developed over many lifetimes, so the goal could be at the beginning, intermediary, or advanced stage of a creative pursuit.

Synthesis and Case Studies

Although there are seven karmic paths to follow, you have the free will to expand your awareness and consciously choose a different path. Your dharmic directions and soul goals are your karmic destiny. And you have free will to fulfill your destiny or to avoid it.

For the first example, let's look at the man destined to fulfill his dharma in government. He may have developed his leadership abilities over many lifetimes. In this life, the family and environment into which he was born and educated are karmic. Because his dharma is governmental leadership, in addition to responding to his own inner nature, he responds to the voice of his country and the direction of a greater whole in accepting leadership.

This individual was born with a dharmic direction of *government* with a soul goal of *fame or power*—a category which also includes leadership positions. This man has purposely chosen to walk the *balanced karmic path* as a result of a strong Christian upbringing. Because he needs an "electable" background, this also helps him to fulfill his long-term political ambitions.

As another example, let's look at a famous singer who has been addicted to drugs for years. He earned the right in past lives to reincarnate with a soul goal of *fame or power* and a dharmic direction of *creativity*. In his earlier years, he was following the *intermediate* karmic path, but because of his drug addiction is now on the *beginning* path. This singer was given the opportunity to inspire and assist others in numerous ways but chose instead to bury himself in self-indulgence.

His wife is an entirely different story. She is also a singer, but is not as famous as her husband. She came into this life with a soul goal to *provide support*, with a secondary goal of *fame or power*. Her dharmic direction is also *creativity*, and she is currently following a *balanced karmic path*. This woman stood by her husband through his years of addiction and has finally helped him overcome his dependency.

Another case history: Jennie is married, has two children that are nearly grown, and sells real estate professionally. Metaphysics is her primary interest in life, and she is actively involved in a metaphysical organization. Her life revolves around her spiritual interests, and she is on the *harmonious* karmic path. She was born with a *workforce* dharmic direction and a soul goal of attaining *knowledge* in the area of devotion. Outward appearances suggest that Jennie is fulfilling her destiny and enjoying her life.

In another case, Matthew is a thirty-two-year-old freelance screenwriter who lives alone in Venice, California. Although quite talented, he makes little money and experiences excessive frustration because he is unwilling to accept the realities of his profession. Matthew is exploring an *intermediate* karmic path and came into this life with *creativity* as his dharmic direction. His soul goal is to *learn acceptance.* Although he doesn't realize it consciously, he is teaching himself to accept *what is* and all that it means.

Karie is a welfare worker in her early forties and has been divorced three times. Her divorces and the inequality and injustice she experiences in her daily work have caused her to look for deeper meaning in life. As a result, she walks a *balanced* karmic path and is aware that she incarnated with a dharmic direction of *service.* Her primary soul goal is to *achieve inner harmony.* From a higher perspective, she desires to learn to accept all the joy and love that life has to offer while allowing the negativity to flow through her without affecting her.

I'm sure you're seeing how the seven karmic paths, seven dharmic directions, and seven soul goals all interrelate as a blueprint of your general life destiny.

So the question is, *why are you here?*

Reinventing Yourself

In addition to recognizing needed changes, removing blocks, establishing goals, and incorporating the happiness potential of an autotelic (self-fulfilling) personality, it's important to know the qualities of the people who make the time and exert the effort to reinvent themselves. Here are some of the main ones:

1. Commit yourself to values and purpose. Those who reinvent themselves set priorities and are always achieving productively. They know that you must have goals if you want to grow, so they organize their time around the things that matter to them.

   Although you must find joy and fulfillment in the present, your peace of mind, health, survival, and success depend upon your willingness to commit to the future. Regularly remind yourself why you are doing what you're doing, and visualize your goals as if they were already accomplished.

2. You need quiet time alone for introspection, to explore potentials, and to nurture yourself. Schedule regular times to withdraw and listen to your inner voice.

3. To pursue your best options, you must adapt to change. Be open to new perspectives, altered goals, and new

ways of thinking. Distinguish between what is and isn't essential, what will endure from what is temporary.

4. Learn from your stress, failures, misfortunes, conflicts, and disagreements. Discovering what doesn't work can help you to learn what does work. Look for the gift in your problems, view the problems as opportunities, and be confident in the future.

5. Pace yourself. You need more than occasional breaks in routine to reinvent yourself. Make time for travel, vacations, seminars, exercise, vigorous activities, and sabbaticals. Everyone has the same number of hours in the day; we either spend it or waste it. Spending it means to pass time in a specific way. Wasting it means just that. Sometimes, however, the best way to spend time is to do nothing.

6. Always continue to study and learn, remaining focused upon who and what you are becoming.

7. Take the initiative to sustain your relationships with your mate, family and friends. Network information, contacts, and resources.

8. Be concerned with quality, not just quantity.

9. Never remain on a comfortable plateau for very long. Continual challenge is important to maintain happiness and self-esteem.

10. Look internally for your motivation. People tend to be motivated externally or internally. The externally motivated find their enjoyment mostly through contact with friends, acquiring possessions, and improving their physical appearance, and from pleasurable events such as parties, sports events, movies, and concerts.

This momentary pleasure usually only provides relief from boredom. Internally motivated people find fulfillment in creating, learning, and accomplishing, all of which increase self-esteem.

11. Always act in ways that support your self-esteem, because you can only attract into your life what you feel worthy of. Every day, remind yourself that you are worthy and deserving of the very best that life has to offer.

Reinventing yourself is easy. Now all you have to do is decide who you want to become, and do it.

Bodhisattvas

Bodhisattva is a Sanskrit term meaning *one who supports others in achieving enlightenment*. The word is composed of *bodhi*, meaning *perfect wisdom*, and *sattva*, meaning *an intelligent being whose actions make for harmony*. According to Zen, these individuals have reached the point of liberation but have decided not to step off the wheel of reincarnation. Instead, they have chosen to continue incarnating to serve other living beings until all are free.

I contend that once someone becomes involved in metaphysical and New Age learning, they have crossed over into the Bodhisattva phase of their spiritual evolution.

Dick Sutphen created his Bushido Training in the 1970s and taught this course for twenty years. The Bushido logo was his design. The symbol of the Bushido® Training Seminar is Manjusri: the Bodhisattva of Wisdom, riding a lion and holding the sword of wisdom that cuts through delusion.

As a guideline for self-advancement, Masters long ago established Six Perfections and Ten Precepts of moral conduct to accelerate the process of liberation.

The Six Perfections

Bodhisattva is sometimes explained as "someone who practices the six paramitas." The first five perfections (*paramitas* in Sanskrit) are of the mind, including the heart and will. Those who have developed detached mind will have these five and will have experienced liberation. They are then ready for the great adventure of transcendental wisdom.

1. **Giving.** There are three kinds of giving: the giving of materials, the giving of awareness, and the giving of "nonafraidness." Giving materials usually means money, clothes, food, or labor. It is usually directed to churches, temples, causes, or organizations assisting the needy. The giving of awareness means to share awareness that will lead others down the path to liberation. The knowledge should never be forced upon another, but one should always take the time and effort to plant seeds in the minds of those who are receptive. The giving of nonafraidness means to be willing to risk yourself to save others from disaster or misfortune.

2. **Keeping the precepts.** This means to live by the Ten Precepts (see next page). To break the precepts results in karma which must be balanced before we can evolve further spiritually.

3. **Perseverance.** The world includes suffering: separation of loved ones, illness, old age, loneliness, accidents,

guilt, monetary hardship, and unfulfilled desires. Yet we must persevere and rise above the sufferings, physically as well as mentally.

4. **Assiduity.** This means to exert the diligence not to do anything disharmonious and to do everything harmoniously. Nothing is completed without diligence. Because we are part of society, we must work for money, name, power, and position; but as Bodhisattvas, we realize that our real work has nothing to do with these things, and should be directed to creating harmony on this earth.

5. **Meditation.** By going within on a regular basis, you become attuned to that which is not manifest and awaken the true Self, which is the universe.

6. **Transcendental wisdom.** This is wisdom that transcends the knowledge of things and of the mind. It transcends all dualities to become illumination.

The Ten Precepts

1. **Not to kill.** This refers to literal killing, but also to help yourself to really live by developing detached mind.

2. **Not to steal.** This refers to literal stealing, but also to give to others. In Zen, if you don't practice donation (giving), you are stealing from yourself and your own potential illumination.

3. **Not to misuse sexuality.** This means that the person having sex with another must consider his own happiness, that of his companion, and that of the third person who will be most affected by his act. If these

three concerned people can be satisfied, then sex falls within the natural law of human beings.

4. **Not to lie.** This means not to lie to others and also to avoid the lie of pride.

5. **Not to misuse intoxicants.** This means not to be drunken or to harm the health of your body or mind by using intoxicants to excess.

6. **Not to slander.** This means to shun gossip, slander, and verbal abuse of any kind. Be truthful and loving with your words.

7. **Not to insult.** This means never to purposefully hurt someone else with words. They will always come back to you through cause and effect.

8. **Not to covet.** This means not wanting to get more than you need; not being greedy and ungenerous toward others who may be in greater need than yourself.

9. **Not to grow angry.** Anger is always a protection against pain, but once you realize the pain exists only because you allow it to exist, you cease to become angry.

10. **Not to slander the All That Is.** This means to become aware that we are the All.

Hypnosis, Meditation, and Altered States of Consciousness

You are already familiar with altered states, although you may not realize it. You pass through these states at least twice a day: as you awaken in the morning and as you fall asleep at night.

Altered states of consciousness can be explained this way: Researchers have divided brain wave activity into these four levels, based on cycles of activity per second.

Beta. These are of relatively low amplitude, and are the fastest of the four different brain waves. Their frequency ranges from 15 to 40 cycles a second. Beta waves are characteristics of a strongly engaged mind. The beta level is full consciousness.

Alpha. Alpha brain waves are slower and higher in amplitude than beta waves. Their frequency ranges from 9 to 14 cycles per second. They reflect a state of nonarousal, as when someone has completed a task and sits down to rest. Someone reflecting or meditating is usually in an alpha state.

Theta. These are of even greater amplitude and slower frequency. This frequency range is normally between 5 and 8 cycles a second. A person who is daydreaming is often in a theta state.

Delta. Here the brain waves are of the greatest amplitude and slowest frequency. They typically center around a range of 1.5 to 4 cycles per second. They never go down to zero, because that would mean that you were brain-dead. Deep, dreamless sleep would take you down to 2 to 3 cycles a second.

When you use hypnosis, meditation, or sleep programming audio programs, you will probably be in the mid-alpha range. In this stage you are definitely in an altered state, but you will also remain fully aware of all that is going on around you. If someone walks into the room while you are in an alpha-level altered state, you will hear them and sense their presence. However, their presence will probably not affect you.

In an altered state of consciousness, you tend to set aside the conscious mind (which nevertheless still remains connected) and narrowly focus your attention on one thing. You can communicate directly with your subconscious while in an altered state. Suggestions given in this state are nearly 100 times as effective in producing positive change as suggestions given in normal waking consciousness.

Anyone who can concentrate for a few moments can learn self-hypnosis or meditation as a way to alter their state of consciousness. The best hypnosis subjects are strong-willed, intelligent, and imaginative.

There are many overlapping levels of altered states, but for the sake of simplicity they are broken down into three. Note that these levels relate to subjective experience rather than the rate of brain wave vibrations.

Light-level altered state. Your body becomes very relaxed, although you will probably not realize you are in an altered state of consciousness. Most people can achieve this level quite easily. It is adequate for mind programming or explorations if you trust your own mind and are open to the impressions being received.

Medium-level altered state. You become relaxed to the point of losing awareness of your body. You are completely open to suggestion and are able to mentally relive any suggested event. Although you remain aware to some degree of any outside disturbances, they will not distract you.

Deep-level altered state. You become almost entirely unconscious, and chances are you will not be able to remember what transpires during the session unless specifically told to do so. One person in ten achieves this "somnambulist" level.

You cannot be controlled by the person guiding your altered-state experience. Although you may have seen a stage hypnotist convince a man to do a graceful hula dance, the hypnotist was not controlling his subject. Altered states of consciousness are also states of hypersuggestibility, and typically stage hypnotists work with somnambulist (deep-level) subjects who are even more open to suggestion. Once the subject was hypnotized, the stage hypnotist simply expanded their belief system. The subject chose to accept the suggestion and act upon it. He had seen a hula dance or observed one on TV or in a movie, so the knowledge of how to do it was locked away in the memory banks of his subconscious mind. The hypnotist's suggestion expanded the subject's belief system to believe he could do the hula; thus he did.

Directly proposed hypnotic suggestions cannot make you do anything against your morals, religion or self-preservation. If such a suggestion were given, you would either refuse to comply or wake up.

The ego cannot be detached while in an altered state (such as hypnosis), so secrets will not come out, and you won't do anything you would not normally do if you felt comfortable about the situation.

You cannot become dependent upon altered states of consciousness, although it is true many people look forward to their daily hypnosis sessions because they become totally relaxed and awaken refreshed.

Self-hypnosis and meditation are learned techniques for achieving an altered state of consciousness. You do have to work at it, but if you are willing to use a program once a day for three weeks, you become a conditioned subject.

As was shown in the diagram of brain-wave levels, both self-hypnosis and meditation can be used to achieve an altered state of consciousness. (See diagrams 1 and 2.)

According to leading-edge physics research, the use of altered states of consciousness (hypnosis, meditation, sleep programming) can lead to a transformation of nearly every part of your life. Physicist Ilya Prigogine proved this with his Nobel Prize–winning theory of dissipative structures. Now confirmed by other experts, this theory has solved the mystery of why altered states can result in life-changing insights, new behavioral patterns, and the relief of lifelong phobias or ailments.

Here's how the theory works: First, you must understand that human beings are structures. The structure of your body is composed of bone, muscle, and ligaments. Your brain, however, is given structure by the thoughts and memories that dictate your actions. Your mental programming (all your past thoughts, actions, experiences and learning) provides your brain structure.

Prigogine's theory states that complex structures (such as the human brain) require an enormous and consistent flow of energy to maintain their structure. In the brain, that energy is measured as brain wave levels on an EEG machine. The up-and-down pattern of brain wave levels reflects a fluctuation of energy to the brain. The larger the brain wave levels, the larger the fluctuation of energy.

When you are fully awake (in beta consciousness), your brain wave levels would show up on an EEG graph as small, rapid, up-and-down lines (see diagram 1). There is little fluctuation in the level of energy.

Diagram 1. Beta brain waves

Beta waves maintain a fairly constant flow of energy through the brain. The small fluctuations of energy are suppressed by the brain. They are compact and allow little new programming to enter.

When you alter your state of consciousness with hypnosis, meditation, or as happens naturally when you are crossing over into sleep, your brain wave levels shift to alpha or theta (diagram 2). In these altered states, there is a large fluctuation in the level of energy.

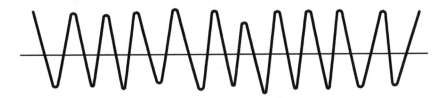

Diagram 2. Alpha and theta waves.

Alpha and theta brain wave levels create large fluctuations of energy through the brain. According to Prigogine, large fluctuations of energy can cause the structure to break apart and reorganize itself into an even more complex and higher form.

That's why suggestions given to an individual in alpha or theta states are so effective in creating change. The new suggestion, dropped into the uneven alpha rhythms like a pebble in a pond, creates a ripple effect through the stretched brain waves, tearing apart old programming and creating new behaviors and viewpoints. Your brain has broken down its old programming and reorganized it into new, more complex, and usually more meaningful forms.

When this shift occurs, you may become aware of information about your life and goals that the old structure of memories and programming kept hidden from you.

You may experience a sudden, powerful insight into an old unsolvable problem, or you may release yourself from the programming effects of a traumatic memory.

Afterwards, it's often difficult to describe the experience. You don't really know why you so firmly believe this is it; this is the block you've been seeking. Sometimes the explanations aren't even logical. For example, there is the case study of Nancy, who had a terrible instance of atopic dermatitis, a chronic skin condition that leaves your skin with itchy, open sores. Practically everything aggravated her condition: too much sun, too much sweat, too much soap.

Nancy had borne the disease since childhood, and doctors told her she could expect to bear it for the rest of her life.

As a last resort, she went into an altered state of consciousness and asked herself, "Why am I creating this skin condition for myself?" The answer she received was: "One of the primary lessons you want to learn in this life is to be sensitive and open to other people. You choose to have a supersensitive exterior—your skin—to remind you to reveal your even more sensitive interior—you true Self. When you do this, your skin condition will disappear."

After coming back to full consciousness, Nancy stated that although logically she shouldn't believe a word of it, for some reason, it felt right. She admitted that she never allowed her true Self to be exposed to others for fear of rejection.

Several months later, Nancy wrote to say that since that session, she had followed her own advice and begun revealing herself to others, who became her friends. Her skin condition had cleared up entirely.

By searching for a solution to an "unsolvable" problem while in an altered state of consciousness, Nancy had caused her mind to reorganize its beliefs about the nature and purpose of her disease. Perhaps in the process of creating new and more complex structures, her mind recognized and used its own ability to heal the body. Or it could be that the skin disease was psychosomatically induced, and thus when her mind reorganized its structures, the purpose for the illness was eliminated.

That's only the beginning of what is possible to achieve through an altered state of consciousness. According to Prigogine's theory, there's an added bonus: each transformation makes the next one likelier! That's because every time you trigger a collapse of memory or data structures, your brain reorganizes its structures into even more complex and more highly organized forms. As a result, it requires even more energy to maintain those structures. And those structures are even more vulnerable to fluctuations of energy. Basically, the more complex a structure is, the more unstable it is, and the easier it is to trigger the next transformation. Hence every time you successfully use an altered state of consciousness to solve a problem, program a new ability, or achieve insights, you increase your chance of success the next time. That's when the miracles begin.

What Can You Expect?

First, you can expect altered state of consciousness programming to accelerate your comprehension and learning skills. Your self-assurance and concentration abilities will increase, as will your intuition. Another major benefit is added willpower and motivation. Some specific results you can expect in different areas of your life are:

Career. Altered states provide the ultimate methodology for understanding and releasing your self-imposed blocks to success. These methods will give you the confidence and charisma you need to improve your sales figures, pitch your ideas successfully, or become a more effective manager. Altered state of consciousness programming can shorten the time it takes you to learn a new skill or earn your next promotion.

Social skills. If remembering people's names is important to you, you can learn how to do it through altered states. It can also increase your confidence when meeting people, improve your public speaking skills, and increase your intuitive ability to understand people.

Bad habits. One of the most common and effective uses of altered state programming is to overcome bad habits such as smoking and overeating. Other bad habits that yield to programming are nail biting, excessive drinking, and nervous habits.

Self-improvement. Altered states are highly effective in improving your own inner reality. This is the ultimate technique for eliminating tension and stress, creating a positive attitude, or increasing peace of mind.

Psychic activity. Altered states are the most effective known methodology for encouraging psychic activity, Higher Self awareness, ESP experiments, psychic input receiving, or vision induction. This process can be extremely successful, because it can be directed to a consciously alert individual who is exploring at the alpha, theta, and delta levels. The resulting "communications" or "impressions" are usually quite vivid.

Most people who inquire about altered states are interested in one or more of the following:

1. Overcoming a problem
2. Accomplishing an objective
3. Having an experience

Altered states of consciousness are certainly no magic wand, but when used correctly, they can give you an edge. They can help you to open all the necessary doors as you proceed towards your goals.

Let Go of Fear

You probably wonder why you are here on the earth and what you are supposed to be doing with the time you have. Wonder no more. Your earthly purpose is to cast away your delusions. Beneath your fearful programming, you are an enlightened soul. The way to liberate yourself is to cast away your delusions, so you can more fully realize what you already are.

If you believe in reincarnation, you may be able to see that we have all reincarnated with the same earthly purpose: to learn to let go of fear and express unconditional love. When I say *fear*, I'm talking about the whole range of neurotic, fear-based emotions such as prejudice, jealousy, hate, envy, possessiveness, greed, blame, resentment, repression, and resistance, plus fears of intimacy, abandonment, commitment, and success, as well as addictions, dependencies, obsessions, and passions. They aren't serving us. They keep us earthbound, reincarnating again and again until we get it right . . . until we learn to let go and integrate these fears.

If you want to know your karma in this life, just look at your fears. Know too that your fears are illusions resulting from old programming (both in this life and past lives).

They are delusions. To summarize your earthly purpose in just four words: *cast away your delusions!*

When you liberate yourself by casting away your delusions, you can come to realize who you already are: an enlightened soul, a spiritual being in a physical body.

Your earthly task is to attain freedom *of* the self as well as freedom *from* the self. Living in the United States, we all have freedom *of* the self, but freedom *from* the self would be a matter of integrating all the fear-based emotions.

Express unconditional love. This a matter of accepting other human beings without trying to change them to be the way you want them to be—without expectations, blame, or trying to control. It is a matter of being compassionate.

Soul Callings

One way your soul prompts you to do what you're destined to do is with what I call *soul callings*. At some point you were called to do what you do today. You can also view this as living out your karma or dharma, which needs to be fulfilled.

Calls come in a variety of forms, which point us in new directions, showing us what our soul needs to experience. Although sometimes they're not easy to decipher, calls point us toward action.

Callings can ask questions such as, "What's right for me?" and "Where am I willing to be led?" And callings will keep surfacing until you deal with them. Sigmund Freud called them "repetition compulsions." In his book *Callings*, Gregg Levoy says that all calls lead to some sacrifice; if you're unwilling to make sacrifices, you can end up losing a great deal more than whatever you might have sacrificed in the beginning.

One of the first places to look for a call is any area of your life where there is friction. As in nature, friction occurs where changes are taking place, or trying to take place. Calls may pursue you in your dreams. Or in a physical symptom, such as a pain in your back, signaling that you are carrying too much responsibility. Or maybe as a song that keeps surfacing. Or maybe you have an ongoing fantasy.

Callings pull people together. When your call relates to others, examine your longings. (Careful here: lust and longings could be two different things.) If you want to explore your callings, you must be willing to be shaken up, to submit to potential discomfort in order to reap the blessings of growth or greater happiness. This stress often generates breakthroughs, as crisis can point you toward new opportunities.

Maybe your call is fated—predestination. Mythologist Joseph Campbell said, "Fate leads those who will, and those who won't, it drags." Campbell spoke of calls as ongoing experiences that hint of our hungers. He urged us to recognize them and listen to them. "The great sacrilege," he said, "in terms of the soul's intensity, is inadvertence . . . or not being alert." In other words, you are not awake!

More often than not, when we resist callings, the result is a reduction of our life force. Our soul shivers and suffers.

We need to understand something about security: it isn't secure! The whole concept of security is contrary to this central fact: *Existence = Life changes.* Although we may want to avoid the sacrifices that are invariably part of fulfilling a call, when we avoid change, we isolate ourselves from living.

Part 2
PRACTICAL APPLICATIONS

The chapters in this section show how to put the principles of part 1 into practice to deal with everyday problems. Many chapters include suggestions for specific actions.

The Care and Feeding of Beliefs

Beliefs generate your thoughts and emotions, which create all your experiences. These beliefs are the result of two things: your present-life programming, resulting from experiences and influences such as parents, church, and society, and past-life programming, resulting in fear-based beliefs that generate self-defeating blocks to attaining happiness and success.

A negative belief is obviously based on fear, but positive beliefs can also be based on fear, and it is important to realize which of them are. Look at some common beliefs that appear to be positive yet are fear-based: You believe your country is the greatest in the world; you believe in the goodness of God; that your mate is faithful; in the loyalty of your friends, in job security. To believe otherwise is fearful. You may even believe UFOs are abducting people or that the Harmonic Convergence inaugurated a new age. But you don't know any of these things for sure. You may be willing to stake your life on what you believe, but your faith doesn't make the belief valid.

Beliefs are not buried deep in the subconscious mind. They are part of our conscious awareness; they just go unexamined because they've been accepted as facts. But there are few facts in life. What we accept as reality is primarily constructed of beliefs about the way things are and ideas about how they should be.

It's easy to recognize your surface beliefs about such things as religion and politics, but I'm talking about core beliefs—who and what you are and how that relates to your success, weight, health, relationships or lack of relationships, career, and everything else central to your existence.

For example, you believe you can only reach a certain level of success, so that's as successful as you are. You believe your body is fat, so you are. If you change your belief, your subconscious programming changes, and your body weight will align with the new programming. Hypnosis and subliminal and sleep programming tapes, which are so popular today, do only one thing: they change old beliefs by programming the subconscious mind with new beliefs.

Self-processing of resentments related to your beliefs can also be valuable. A universal law says you cannot become what you resent. This law is absolute, because you always live up to your self-image. As an example, let's say you are overweight; when you see someone with a beautiful body, you make a snide comment such as, "All beauty and no brains." In so doing, you doom yourself to being overweight, because if you believe people with beautiful bodies have no brains, you will never allow yourself to have a beautiful body. You certainly don't want to be brainless.

As another example, let's say you are actively seeking financial success, but at a stoplight, when you pull up beside a Rolls-Royce, you look over and think, "Rich people are such snobs." Now you are ensuring that you will never be rich. You wouldn't allow yourself to have the self-image of a snob.

Here are some other examples of assumed limitations and faulty beliefs: "I'm a $25,000 a year commissioned sales rep, but I'm not capable of being a $75,000 a year man." "If I'm direct and honest in my communications, I'll probably lose all my friends." "I'd really love to have a good relationship, but it isn't possible being married to Fred."

Usually, assumed limitations and faulty assumptions are directly related to your self-image and the size of your vision. Until you become aware of your mental limitations, it is unlikely you'll do anything to rise above them.

Free Yourself from Limiting Beliefs

We can lock onto old beliefs because we want to protect ourselves from change. Here's an example: A hypnotist counselor has a new client who comes in claiming that he is dead. The hypnotist tells the man, "You've heard, haven't you, that dead men don't bleed?"

"Yes," the client replies.

The hypnotist takes a pin and pokes the man in the arm, making him bleed. "What do you say now?" asks the hypnotist.

"What do you know?" the client says. "Dead men do bleed."

Your disharmonious beliefs are like walls surrounding you and restricting your life. If you want to tear down the walls, first you must recognize that they exist and that you are not free. You can't change what you don't recognize.

Once you are aware of your undesirable beliefs, you can begin the process of reinvention by taking the following steps:

1. Examine the belief in relationship to reality. The belief needs to be tested against *what is*.

2. If you don't know the source of the belief, it will probably serve you to find it with regressive hypnosis.

3. Begin altered-state reprogramming using self-hypnosis or prerecorded tapes.

4. If you know that the belief isn't logical as it relates to your current life, and you know the cause, start forgiving yourself and anyone else involved in the experience that created the belief. Include the following mantra as part of your daily meditation or programming sessions: *I know the cause of this situation, and I now release the effect. I forgive myself and everyone else involved, and in so doing I release the effect and liberate myself.* Chant it over and over in the altered state as you visualize yourself free of the effect.

Realize that limitations and assumptions are self-imposed beliefs. They are not real.

The next step to rising above the effects of restrictive thinking is to become clear on your intent. Exactly what do you want, why do you want it, and what are you willing to do to get it?

The Mistake of Blame

Blame is incompatible with the acceptance of karma and cause and effect as the basis of your reality. Assuming you set it up for yourself to experience exactly what you are experiencing as an opportunity to learn, then how can there ever be anyone to blame?

If you sincerely want your life to work better, it is time to give up all blame, anger, resentment, hostility, and desire for revenge. You and you alone are responsible for everything that ever happened to you. Self-pity is negative programming. To create a positive future, begin to program positive input.

It is easier to be a victim and blame others for your circumstances than it is to take responsibility for your life. From a metaphysical perspective, blame is incompatible with reincarnation and karma. We are here on earth to learn, and we set up the circumstances as tests to judge our level of awareness. Since you assigned yourself your lessons, there is no one but yourself to blame for anything you've ever experienced.

Also, if you think about it, you will realize that anytime you blame anyone for anything, you are expressing self-pity. Think about all the people who have victimized you:

your mate who divorced you, your friend who betrayed you, your business partner who ripped you off. You can't blame them. They supplied the opportunities you needed to experience. Thank them. Release them.

From a human-potential perspective, blame is self-pity. Relate this to your life, and you'll realize how true it is. Self-pity is also negative programming of your subconscious mind, so it is doubly destructive.

Action Required

Realize the futility of blame. You are the only one harmed by the illusion. The acceptance of self-actualizing metaphysical philosophy will transform the way you experience the negativity.

Negative Payoff

A negative payoff is a situation in which you say you want something to be different than it is, but consciously or subconsciously, you block the desired goal because there is a payoff in maintaining the status quo. A good example of this was a woman in a seminar who said she desired to be wealthy. She worked hard and used programming techniques to support her goals. Yet when I began to process her, it became obvious she was subconsciously blocking her own success out of love for her father. If she allowed herself to "show him up," he would be hurt, and she would experience the guilt.

In another case, a woman claimed she wanted to find a husband. But she was extremely overweight and did nothing to make herself more attractive. During processing, she said a mate would be possessive—restricting her activities and complicating her life. "I'm not too fond of fixing meals on schedule, or washing and ironing either," she added. Obviously, no matter how much she talked about wanting to get married, there was a bigger payoff in remaining single.

Action Required

Explore your goals and desires. Ask yourself two questions: "If I get what I say I want, what will change?" and "What are the potential undesirable changes?" The negative payoffs will be in the answers to the second question.

Masks or Acts

Whenever you wear masks, you are attempting to avoid pain. You think the real you isn't adequate enough, or impressive enough, or kind enough, or loving enough, so you pretend to be more than you are. Maybe you're afraid of hurting someone's feelings, so you wear a nice mask. Or you're insecure about your job, so you wear a sincere and dependable mask. A gregarious mask is good for deflecting real contact, avoiding intimacy, or hiding insecurity. There are thousands of masks.

Masks are repressions, which are a form of fear. There is no way to successfully repress who you are. It's like holding a rubber life raft under water. As long as you're willing to exert effort, you can do it, but eventually you're going to get tired, and the raft will surface. A man represses his anger with his wife but takes it out on his employees. A woman wears a fake smile all day at work; her repression takes the form of an ulcer. For years a man checks his emotional desires, and the repression manifests as cancer. Repressed feelings will always come out.

Action Required

There are three ways to generate change in a human being:

1. Add something to their life, such as people, things, environment, awareness, programming, or challenges.
2. Subtract something from their life—again, people, things, environment, challenges.
3. Get the person to be who they really are. This is transcendental change. Accepting what is in yourself is the beginning of transformation, because you can't change what you don't recognize.

Here are some steps to help you clear yourself of masks:

1. Understand why you wear the mask. What is the fear behind the false face?
2. Decide if the reason you wear it is valid anymore. Often it isn't.
3. Analyze the cost of wearing your mask. How is the resulting repression manifesting in your life?
4. Realize that all you have to do to remove your mask is be direct and honest in your communications with others.

Incompatible Goals and Values

If your goals and values are not compatible, you will either subconsciously block yourself from achieving your goals or you'll change your values to make them consistent with your goals. A third possibility is that you'll destroy one or the other in the process. As an example, if your wife and family are your highest value, and your goal is to become a manufacturer's representative covering a five-state territory, your value and goal are inconsistent. Your work would necessitate travel, allowing minimal home life.

Action Required

Recognize the incompatible goals and values. List your goals, one to ten, with the most important at the top. Do the same with your values. Any great separation on the list will indicate that you need to rethink one or the other in order to resolve or avoid conflict.

Mirroring

The positive or negative qualities you react to in others reflect the same qualities within you. Other people are a mirror for you; if you are aware, you can learn from the mirror. If you see fear in someone else, you're recognizing fear within yourself. If you think someone is selfish and it bothers you, be aware there is selfishness within you. Any quality in another person that really bothers or attracts you exists within yourself as well.

Action Required

Examine your reactions to others by searching yourself for the corresponding traits. If your reaction is negative, it is rooted in a fear, which you are here on earth to resolve.

See the people you dislike as mirrors instead of adversaries.

Fear

Fear is a big word. All disturbances between human beings, large or small, interpersonal or international, are rooted in fear. Fear means all the negative emotions such as anger, selfishness, jealousy, prejudice, hate, repression, envy, possessiveness, greed, anxiety, guilt, insecurity, depression, inhibitions, vanity, malice, resentment, and blame. The fears work against your spiritual evolution, and they can paralyze you, keeping you from acting when you need to act—keeping you from making a growth choice when it would be in your best interest.

Action Required

Discover the cause of the fear if possible. Next, work to rise above the effects of the fear by examining it in the light of reality. When measured logically and from a self-actualized, metaphysical perspective, the fear will prove to be a delusion. Nonetheless, if the fear is caused by repressed anger (as is often the case with anxiety, guilt, and depression), it's often necessary to express your true feelings as a first step in releasing the anger. In other fear-based situations, it is of value to confront the fear by gathering the courage to act despite your desire to play it safe.

The Need to Be Right

Your subconscious mind is a memory bank and operates very much like a computer. It's programmed for survival and for you to be "right." Everything you consider saying or doing is quickly run through your data banks, comparing the present to related past experiences. Your computer then approves your actions as compared to the past, for in the past you survived.

Computers are logically programmed machines and cannot be wrong. To be wrong is a malfunction. Similarly, if your subconscious computer allows you to be wrong, its survival is threatened. So the only way it can work is to make you feel correct. It doesn't reason, and it doesn't care if you get what you want out of life. It just needs to be right to protect itself, even if you lose the game.

The result of your subconscious computer running the show is your current life just the way it is. Your computer says that it's OK to live your life as you do in comparison to the past, and it refers to its memory banks for guidance and justification. Some of this is good: it causes you to look both ways before running out into the street. But some of this programming creates problems for you. If you starved to death in a past life, you may be programmed to over-eat in an attempt to survive now. If success in a former incarnation led to self-indulgence and ruination, you may be programmed to avoid success this time around. If you didn't make enough money to feed your children in a previous incarnation, you might be a workaholic today.

In such situations, your subconscious computer is out of alignment with conscious reality. Nevertheless, the only way it can function is to be right and to make you feel right about your decisions. Why? Because it wants *you* to survive so *it* can survive. It doesn't care if you get what you want out of life; it just needs to be right in order to protect itself. So what happens? Your subconscious computer gets to be right, and you lose the game.

A friend of mine I'll call Dan was married to a wonderful lady. Dan had to be right; he always had all the answers. Every time his wife opened her mouth, Dan would correct her. After five years of this, his wife filed for a divorce, because she was tired of being wrong all the time. Dan didn't want the divorce, but for five years, he had gotten to be right and now he's lost the game.

A man named Jim used to come to all the seminars I conducted in California and Arizona. He always listened intently, frequently shaking his head negatively throughout the day. At the end of each seminar, he would come up and tell me that he could conduct a far better seminar. I let him be right, acknowledging his "rightness" by saying, "Yes, Jim, I understand that you think that." He got to be right, and I continued to win the game by collecting his seminar fees.

No matter what the situation, most people are programmed to be right, and will instantly go on "tilt" if you challenge their rightness. Consequently, it makes sense to let others be right . . . while you win the game. If your only goal is to get to be right, you would be wise to rethink your priorities.

Our seminar coordinator used to keep several boxes of tissue to pass out to participants who cry during past-life regression. One time she realized, just prior to my tear-inducing "victim/bad guy" regression, that she had forgotten the tissues. Running quickly to the hotel's housekeeping department, she discovered the door was locked, so she went to the assistant manager. "I need some tissues immediately!" she demanded.

Affronted by her demand, the assistant manager resorted to rightness. "I'm sorry, but housekeeping is closed. You should have asked sooner. There is absolutely no way I can help you now."

The coordinator was about to push the issue when she remembered my talks about rightness. "Yes, I do understand that," she said. "But in a few minutes a lot of people are going to be crying in the seminar, and I don't have any tissues for them. What can we do about it?"

The manager, upon being allowed to be right, could concentrate upon the problem. He "robbed" several hotel bathrooms of their boxes of tissues.

When my son, Travis, was younger, I didn't have time to pack his big-wheel tricycle to take on a plane trip. When I presented it to the baggage check-in, the clerk said, "You can't check it through like this. It has to be in a shipping carton."

If I had challenged him, he wouldn't have backed down. Instead I said, "I know you're right, but my son really wants to have his bike on vacation. Isn't there anything we can do?" The big-wheel traveled to our destination in an airline dog transport cage.

To give up being right means cutting some of the connections between you and the robot portion of your totality. But when you stop attempting to be right, you avoid many hassles and have extra time to do more productive things.

Always be aware that the other guy (or gal) needs to be right. His computer functions that way: unless you let him be right, his survival is threatened, and there will be trouble.

So, remembering that your goal is to win the game, quickly allow him or her to be right with a phrase such as, "Yes, I understand that." It's so simple, and you're not giving up a thing, but it is enough to take them off "tilt." Their computer's survival will no longer be threatened, and they can then concentrate on the problem.

Action Required

Learn to be aware of your programming so you can detach from the buttons that cause you to act like a robot. A robot has no choice in the way it acts. It has wiring and circuits which are set so that when a button is pushed, it reacts according to programming.

In many areas of your life, you are programmed the same way. When your button is pushed, you need to be right. Even if you're not, you'll find some way to twist it around to justify yourself. Only those with enlightened awareness of how human beings work understand this, but winning the game of life is far more satisfying than getting to be right.

Expectations

Expectations of a forthcoming experience will seldom serve you, because if the experience doesn't live up to your expectations, you'll be disappointed or unable to enjoy it for what it is.

Expectations of other people will never serve you. Whenever you expect someone else to be the way you want them to be, you're likely to be disappointed. No one can change someone else, nor can they expect another person to be anything other than what they are. When you insist that someone act according to your rules, you are trying to force them to repress who they really are. Even if they comply, long-term repression is impossible, so the forced change will not last, or it will result in new eruptions of unsatisfactory behavior.

Action Required

Attain a self-actualized perspective of the futility of expectations. Since it is impossible to change people, accept them as they are without resisting *what is*.

Clarity of Intent

The primary reason people are not as happy or successful as they desire to be is that they are not clear about their intent. In other words, they don't know exactly what they want. If you don't know what you want, how do you expect to get it?

When I process people in my seminars—even when people appear to be clear about what they want in life—their confusion becomes obvious. All too often their wants are based upon what they think they should want, or what they think their friends or family want. Maybe they feel their real wants are greedy, so they disguise them. Others feel their real wants are irresponsible or unrealistic, so they won't admit to them.

Action Required

1. To unleash the unlimited power of your mind, you have to be honest with yourself about what you want.
2. Discover what is blocking you from getting what you want. It will be one of three things: a subconscious fear, a negative payoff, or a totally unrealistic goal.

3. Decide what you are willing to pay to get what you want. The price will be one or more of the following: time, effort, money, or sacrifice.

Once you have this awareness, either you will decide to accomplish your goal or you will accept that it isn't really what you want. Either way, your life will work better, for you will no longer be dealing with illusion.

Lack of Motivation or Aliveness

Aliveness is real enjoyment in doing what you do. It's the excitement and exhilaration that make you glad to be alive. It's the joy, stimulation, and pleasure that make life worth living.

The best way I've found to generate aliveness and motivation is to get someone to do what they really want to do. What you want to do is always your best option in life, because life appears to be set up for you to get what you want—if you dare to want it. So when you are making choices, choose what you want most, not which choice appears to make the most sense.

Action Required

To overcome lack of aliveness and motivate yourself, get involved in what really interests you. You must have strength-producing activity in your life, or you will become depressed. Your mind will never allow your life to become too boring and mundane without doing something to make it more interesting. The problem is, it might generate difficulties in your life.

Lack of Self-Discipline

Self-discipline is the basis of all self-change. It isn't about self-denial or self-restriction. In the context of success, it means self-determination. Perseverance in action is the very basis of success, because it is the way you direct your time, energy, and resources to manifest your desires. Self-discipline is the one factor common to all successful self-made people. It means you do what you need to do when you need to do it and stop doing what doesn't work.

Action Required

If you are confused about goals and values and you lack clarity of intent, you will also lack self-discipline. So first, reevaluate those factors. Lack of self-discipline also manifests in procrastination, avoiding, or indefinitely postponing chores or projects you dislike doing. If there is no way around what needs to be done, and you can't delegate the work to someone else, then you must accept *what is* and handle it.

Large projects can be especially overpowering, but good planning can help you to get going. Direct your time and energy to maximize your efforts and do the job one step at a time until it's done. Remind yourself that you are doing the job because you freely choose to do it, not because you are being forced to. (In reality, you don't *have* to do anything.) It may also help to begin controlling the negative thoughts that are influencing your actions.

Misplaced Passion

Misplaced passion is a matter of having great energy and enthusiasm for something that doesn't serve you or offers little potential for success. Example: You love motorcycles more than anything in the world. You read everything ever written about motorcycles, you spend your evenings and weekends riding motorcycles, and any remaining spare time is spent talking with friends about motorcycles. At the same time, you have little or no energy for your business, a small travel agency. You know if you were to spend some of your energy investigating unique travel aspects and promoting them to potential customers, your business would improve. But you don't do it.

Action Required

First, explore the emotional needs your misplaced passion is fulfilling. In the motorcycle situation, it might be the sense of freedom you experience on the bike, or the satisfaction to be found in tinkering with a precise mechanical object. This being the case, there might be ways to fulfill these needs as a part of your travel business.

Ideally, by following your passion you can parlay your passionate energy into success.

Maybe in the above case, you'd be better off selling your travel agency and opening a motorcycle shop. If there are already too many motorcycle shops in your town, you might have to move to another town. If that isn't a viable option, you'll have to accept the success level of your travel agency while knowing you have the potential to improve it.

Another option: you might try to integrate your business and passion by creating motorcycle safaris, or arranging European motorcycle vacations. If this isn't possible and your business demands more attention, you'll have to find the self-discipline to sacrifice some of the time you spend on your motorcycle and apply it to your business instead.

Part 3
ISSUES IN HYPNOSIS

Much of Dick's work was focused on working as a hypnotherapist. This section contains writings dealing with some specific issues that come up in hypnosis, particularly for subjects.

Body Position in Hypnosis

Try to pick a time and place for hypnosis when you will not be interrupted and a place where it is quiet. You may sit in a comfortable chair or lie down in bed. If you are sitting, place both feet flat on the floor and your hands on your legs. If you're lying down, do not cross your legs. Weight can be exaggerated during hypnosis. Place your hands at your sides.

The lying down position is best unless it causes you to fall into a normal sleep. Avoid using your audio program when you are very tired. The program will condition your subconscious mind, and you don't want to condition falling asleep when going into a hypnotic state. If you fall asleep two times while in the prone position, continue further sessions in a sitting position for a few days. If you don't do this, your subconscious will quickly become programmed to fall asleep every time you listen to audio programming.

The subconscious mind contains all of the memories of this life and any other lives you have lived, but it has very little reasoning power. Thus it can be easily programmed contrary to your conscious desires, unless you know how to work with it. There is no danger in falling asleep while using a hypnosis program; it is only the sleep habit pattern established in the subconscious that is to be avoided. If you wear contact lenses and normally remove them when you go to sleep, take them out before doing a hypnosis session.

Deep Breathing

Before you enter an altered state, yoga or meditative breathing should be used to relax your body and mind. Take the position you will be using during the session (sitting or lying down), and set your audio player beside you so you will need only reach over to press the play button.

Now take a deep breath... let it out slowly between slightly parted lips. When you think the breath is all the way out, pull your stomach in to push the breath even further out, and further out. It's best to take at least five to ten of these deep breaths before you go into an altered state of consciousness.

Use visualization. Really feel yourself in the situation you desire, or having what you are desiring. Spend time feeling what it's like to have this in your life. The secret to receiving in an altered-state is *trust*. Trust what you are feeling and experiencing. You may be receiving impressions as a fantasy, as thoughts or feelings, or you may hear an inner voice. Trust how you receive impressions. The more you do this exercise, the better you will get at programming your subconscious mind through the altered state process.

How to Receive Vivid Impressions

About 85 percent of those using self-hypnosis and meditation techniques to explore the unknown will easily receive vivid impressions. The remaining 15 percent must be convinced to trust themselves. They expect subjective input to be perceived in a particular way, and when their experience doesn't live up to the expectation, they block themselves. Their belief destroys their experience, for they expect to receive perfect dreamlike impressions, and that simply isn't the way it works for most people.

Everyone can receive in hypnosis: it is a simple process of self-trust. The experience is different for everyone, though, and this seems to be what some people find frustrating. The primary misconception is that the experience isn't real unless you can see a vivid picture in your mind.

Though many people receive visual or fantasy-like impressions, others simply perceive thoughts or feelings. Some people see nothing at all, and yet they are able to relate numerous details. Others get the impression that during the regression they are making it all up, even though later their experiences have been historically documented. You have to be willing to trust your mind and your impressions.

Most people perceive as if they were creating a fantasy in their own mind. Think about the last time you mentally relived an argument or experienced a sexual fantasy. You imagined the situation and became emotionally involved in it, yet you also remained fully aware of your surroundings; you realized you were creating the fantasy.

Now stop and reread these last few sentences. They sum up the way you will probably feel while receiving past-life impressions in an altered state.

There are, of course, many other ways to perceive. For example, some people receive single pictures, like watching slides viewed through a slide projector. Others hear a voice. Some become emotionally involved, as if they were actually reliving the experience, while at other times you'll be detached, perceiving the events as an observer.

Dick was a light-level subject: in an altered state, he was fully aware of all that was going on around him. He had hundreds of past-life experiences in which he perceived vivid impressions that were later documented historically. Like most people, Dick received a thought or fantasy impressions. He believed at the time he was making up the entire experience, but he eventually learned to trust the input received in hypnosis.

Stanford Research Institute made the national news when its researchers proved that everyone is psychic. Under the auspices of the institute, scientists Russell Targ and Harold Puthoff conducted extensive remote viewing experiments under laboratory-controlled conditions. The format of the experiment was to ask test subjects to psychically perceive distant locations that had been chosen at random. Test subjects were told, "You have permission to be psychic. In fact, we expect it of you." Subjects were also told to trust the impressions they received, even though they would probably feel they were making it up. The successful results of the study proved that we have the ability to project our minds to, and accurately perceive, distant locations. It is not difficult to develop psychic ability, although it can be difficult to trust ourselves.

When some people close their eyes, they claim to see only blackness. In the Stanford tests, blackness was not acceptable. Researchers claimed that impressions were bound to come through the blackness if the test subjects only trusted their minds.

Now let's do a short exercise that will illustrate this concept.

Close your eyes and imagine your bathroom at home. Perceive it clearly; create every detail in your mind. Ask yourself where the sink is located, and the toilet, the shower, the tub . . . what do the flooring and walls look like? Where were the towels and toiletries when you last saw the room? Close your eyes and answer all these questions.

Let's do one more exercise. Once again close your eyes and imagine an American Indian riding a horse. You've seen this image many times on TV or in movies, so draw upon these memories to create a vivid mental image of the Indian on horseback. Create the environment in which the Indian is riding. Do this for about thirty seconds.

You have just perceived impressions through the blackness of your closed eyes. You made them up, and they appeared in your mind. This is the very least you should perceive in subjective explorations, such as past-life regression or remote viewing. Just as you saw your bathroom with your inner eyes, you can see your past lives, future potentials, or hidden information in exactly the same way—and probably with much more intensity.

Some people may challenge the validity of the exercise, saying that the mental pictures of their bathroom are being pulled from their memories. That's right: of course, that's what's happening. Everything is recorded in the memory banks of your subconscious mind—every thought, every action, every deed from this life you are now living and any other previous incarnation. You absolutely have the power and ability to perceive them all in vivid detail.

Probably the single most valuable receiving tip is, trust the very first thought that pops into your mind. This is what most psychics do. There is no little red light that goes on in a psychic's mind when she is receiving a psychic impression. She simply learns to trust that initial impression and let it unfold naturally. If she begins to analyze, intellectualize, or question, she loses the impression. So try not to question the process while you're receiving. Don't question whether you're perceiving valid impression or making them up. You'll have plenty of time for that after the session.

One of the primary questions that comes up is: "How do I know that what I'm receiving is valid?" There is no simple answer. Rather than proving or disproving results, why not judge by the effect on your life? Does the information you received explain a situation, decreasing your anxiety? Does the awareness resolve an old problem? Does it make you feel better about yourself or someone else? It's your belief, and you wouldn't receive a positive benefit if the information weren't valid on some level.

Some people judge the validity of their altered state experience by researching its historical accuracy or through other forms of verification. If the impressions are prophetic and the prediction is fulfilled, there is little doubt about the validity of the information. In the final analysis, you are the judge of your own experience.

How Many Things Can I Work On at Once?

Once you've discovered how extremely effective hypnosis, meditation, and sleep programming are, you'll probably want to begin to work on many changes at once. Try to refrain from doing this. You'll have more immediate results by concentrating your efforts on one or two primary directions until you have achieved your goals, then moving on to a new area of programming.

In some situations, however, you can work on several related things at one time. For example, you might choose to develop your concentration abilities at the same time you're using a prerace hypnosis audio program right before a marathon, and feet and leg relaxation hypnosis right after a race.

One excellent combination would be to program your short- and-long-term goals along with health and healing suggestions. As your goals change, you can also change your programming.

Some people have reported using an audio program ten times a day. This is entirely unnecessary. One daily session is adequate, and two is the maximum suggested.

Some short-term programming examples: stopping smoking, losing weight, being patient, developing concentration, expanding creativity, and developing sports abilities.

Long-term programming examples: making a major career change, owning your own business, creating financial success, healing, or writing.

Retaining Your Impressions

Subjective impressions received in altered states are often like dreams in that they quickly fade. For this reason, you might want to have a pencil and paper beside you when you awaken so you may quickly write down the highlights of the session. You might also speak into a voice recorder, so you can keep your eyes closed and verbally commit your experience to a voice file while the images are still fresh in your mind.

Many people use voice recorders, leaving them on while they listen to the audio hypnosis program. They then speak up and verbalize their impressions as they are occurring. The result is the same as a directed past-life regression. Speaking up will not bring you out of an altered state; in fact, it's a great solution for keeping you focused on the input if you tend to drift off or fall asleep.

Once you are fully conditioned, you may sometimes go into an altered state without remembering anything until you awaken. If you are opening your eyes on the count of five, you are not going off into a natural sleep. You may actually be too good a subject and are doing what we call "tripping" or drifting in and out.

There are several solutions. First, try sitting up against a wall or in a chair while exploring in an altered state. You won't be quite as comfortable, but this may help keep you from tripping.

If you are simply going too deep, don't do any deep breathing before the induction.

Once you have become conditioned, you may also want to shorten the induction by imagining a wave of relaxation moving from your toes to your head. Another technique is to keep yourself fully conscious during the initial part of the induction. On the hypnosis programs, begin participating at the second countdown of seven (if there are two); on all other programs, begin to participate about halfway through the induction.

Other techniques that may keep you from falling asleep or tripping out: if you're familiar with yoga postures, do about fifteen minutes of them before going into trance. A natural "upper" that will help keep you alert is a mixture of vitamin E and honey. Combine the exercises with the mixture about twenty minutes before you go into trance. This will give you a "speed" effect that will last about four hours. The yoga, honey, and E combined will keep you extremely alert. The honey instantly puts sugar into your system, and the E extends the oxygen. Don't use this technique if you've been drinking alcohol, for it will work in reverse—as a downer. If you wish to avoid honey, take two super–high quality B complex vitamins at least thirty minutes before you go into hypnosis. B's are fatigue fighters and will help you remain alert.

A small percentage of people sometimes experience the feeling of spinning or swaying while in an altered state—especially towards the completion of the induction. There is nothing to fear: simply give yourself the strong command, "Stabilize!" You are in control, and you can stop the effect.

Headache

Very rarely someone will awaken with a headache that feels like a tight band around the forehead. Although somewhat uncomfortable, it is not a matter for concern and will usually disappear within thirty minutes. The ache can be the result of anxiety about the altered state experience, but those involved in metaphysical investigation feel it is the result of third eye activity and indicates the awakening of psychic abilities. Using altered state techniques often expands extrasensory perception even when the subject isn't trying to be psychic.

Spiritual Healing

Your physical body wants to be well, but your mind often diverts it from this normal condition. Research has shown that it's your state of mind, more than anything else, that determines how healthy you are. Your mind has a great effect on your healing process.

The legendary magus Hermes Trismegistus, said to have lived some time before Moses, is also said to have founded the art of healing. (For further research, read *The Emerald Tablet of Hermes* and *The Kybalion*, which are classic books on Hermetic philosophy.) Hermes states that a negative state of mind is a breeding ground for disease. In other words, most health problems are emotionally induced: they started out mentally and became physical.

The good news is that what your mind has created, your mind can change. I have seen this over and over again. I use the statement, "Wisdom erases karma" to show how you can take charge of your mental and physical life to overcome any karmic obstacles you have put in your path through wisdom and the power of grace.

Everything we experience is karmic, beginning with thoughts we think. From a karmic perspective, you and you alone are responsible for everything that ever happened to you.

When it comes to healing, since you're the cause, you'll ideally be active rather than passive in the healing process.

Forgiveness

Forgiveness is a key factor in healing. Sometimes, to be healed of a mental, emotional or physical problem, an individual needs to resolve a negative relationship or stop blaming themselves or someone else. Forgiveness is key in the healing process.

Explore if there is anyone you need to forgive. If so, work on releasing the energy binding the two of you. In doing this, you free yourself of negativity, which always blocks healing.

Levels of Healing

Healing occurs on four levels, or planes of existence.

1. The highest level is the *spiritual* plane.
2. The *mental* plane is the level of thoughts and mind.
3. The *etheric* plane is the level of emotions.
4. The familiar *physical* plane.

Metaphysics also teaches that there are four energy bodies of man simultaneously coinciding in space.

1. The *physical body*, which exists on the physical plane.
2. The *vital body*, the *etheric double*, which maintains your perfect model for the physical body.

3. The *astral body*, which is able to leave the physical body but is attached to it with the "silver cord" mentioned in the Bible (Ecclesiastes 12:6).

4. The *mental body*, where it all begins. Sometimes called the *causal body*.

Spiritual healing uses the etheric body as a perfect model but considers the importance of all four bodies in activating and maintaining the invisible subtle energy system, including the energy centers known as chakras.

These four bodies all coexist right here in the same space. How can this be? As Albert Einstein showed, matter is energy. This means that all the metal, plastic, and wood surrounding you is not solid. What appears solid is actually made up of swirling molecules temporarily molded in their current patterns and vibrating at rates of "metal," "plastic," or "wood."

Our world and everything in it are not what they appear to be. Nothing is solid; everything is energy. And energy is nonphysical in nature. Your body is energy; your four bodies are all energy.

Cutting-edge physicists are now saying that our reality appears to be more like a thought form than anything else. This fact does not surprise the mystics, who have always said we live in a world of illusion.

Here we are, vibrating within a particular range of frequency, where we see the earth visually. Let's just say it's vibrating at a frequency of 99.5. If we apply this analogy to the other energy bodies, the spiritual body may be vibrating at a frequency of 108.7, while the etheric and mental bodies are vibrating at lower rates. In short, other realities coexist in the same space, but because their frequency is not the same as ours, we do not perceive them, and they do not perceive us.

Energy can affect energy. You and those around you are energy interacting with energy. That's what this reality of ours is all about. Energy learning to harmoniously work with energy is what I call spiritual healing.

The Battle for Your Mind

Persuasion and Brainwashing Techniques
Used on the Public Today

The following is an expanded version of a talk Dick Sutphen delivered at the World Congress of Professional Hypnotists Convention in Las Vegas, Nevada. Although the paper carries a 1984 copyright to protect the contents from unlawful duplication for sale, Dick has invited individuals to make copies and give them to friends or anyone in a position to communicate this information. Since the paper was released, it has been distributed to millions and is currently available on dozens of websites. As a result of this awareness, Dick has been contacted by law enforcement officers, the BBC, and investigative reporters. On numerous occasions, the information has helped to bring public attention to the misuse of conversion tactics.

Some government agencies don't want this information generally known, because the techniques are used in armed forces basic training. Some Christian fundamentalists, cults, and human potential trainings would also prefer that the public remain unaware of how they are recruiting new members.

*   *   *

I'm going to talk about conversion, which is a nice word for brainwashing. Everything I'll share only exposes the surface of the problem. I don't know how the misuse of these techniques can be stopped other than through public awareness. It isn't possible to legislate against what often cannot be detected; and if those who legislate are using these techniques, there is little hope of affecting laws to govern usage.

In talking about mind manipulation, I am talking about my own business. I know it, and I know how effective it can be. I produce hypnosis and subliminal tapes and, in some of my seminars, I use conversion tactics to assist participants to become independent and self-sufficient. But any time I use these techniques, I point out that I am using them, and those attending have a choice to participate or not. They're also aware of the desired result of participation.

To begin, I want to share a basic fact about brainwashing: *in the entire history of man, no one has ever been brainwashed and realized, or believed, that he has been brainwashed.* Those who have been brainwashed will usually passionately defend their manipulators, claiming they have simply been "shown the light" or have been transformed in miraculous ways.

The Birth of Conversion

Any study of brainwashing has to begin with a study of Christian revivalism in eighteenth-century America. Apparently, the clergyman Jonathan Edwards accidentally discovered the techniques during a religious crusade in 1735 in Northampton, Massachusetts. By creating guilt and acute apprehension and increasing the tension, he induced the sinners attending his revival meetings to break down and completely submit. Technically, Edwards was creating conditions that wipe the brain slate clean so that the mind accepts new programming. He would tell those attending, "You're a sinner! You're destined for hell!"

As a result, one person committed suicide, and another attempted suicide. The neighbors of the suicidal converts related that they too were affected so deeply that, although they had found "eternal salvation," they were obsessed with a diabolical temptation to end their own lives.

Once a preacher, cult leader, manipulator, or authority figure creates the brain phrase to wipe the brain slate clean, his subjects are open to new programming. New input, in the form of suggestions, can be substituted for their previous ideas. Because Edwards didn't make his message positive until the end of the revival, many accepted the negative suggestions and acted, or desired to act, upon them.

Charles G. Finney was another Christian revivalist who used the same techniques four years later in mass religious conversions in New York. The techniques are still being used today by Christian revivalists, cults, human-potential training, some business rallies, and the US armed services.

I don't think most revivalist preachers realize they are using brainwashing techniques. Edwards simply stumbled upon a technique that worked, and others have continued to copy it for over two hundred years. And the more sophisticated our knowledge and technology become, the more effective the conversion. I feel strongly that this is one of the major reasons for the increasing rise in Christian fundamentalism, especially the televised variety, while most of the orthodox religions are declining.

The Three Brain Phases

The Christians may have been the first to successfully formulate brainwashing, but we have to look to Ivan Pavlov, the Russian scientist, for a technical explanation. In the early 1900s, his work with conditioning animals opened the door to further investigations with humans. After the revolution in Russia, Lenin was quick to see the potential of applying Pavlov's research to his own ends.

Pavlov identified three distinct and progressive states of transmarginal inhibition. The first is the *equivalent* phase, in which the brain gives the same response to both strong and weak stimuli. Second is the *paradoxical* phase, in which the brain responds more actively to weak stimuli than to strong. Third is the *ultraparadoxical phase*, in which conditioned responses and behavior patterns turn from positive to negative or from negative to positive. With the progressions through each phase, the degree of conversion becomes more effective and complete.

The ways to achieve conversion are many and varied, but the usual first step in religious or political brainwashing is to work on the emotions of an individual or group until they reach an abnormal level of anger, fear, excitement, or nervous tension. The progressive result of this mental condition is to impair judgment and increase suggestibility. The more this condition can be maintained or intensified, the more it compounds. Once catharsis, or the first brain phase, is reached, the complete mental takeover becomes easier. (Catharsis is a purging of repressed emotions.) Existing mental programming can be replaced with new patterns of thinking and behavior.

Other often used physiological weapons to modify normal brain functions are fasting, radical or high-sugar diets, physical discomforts, regulation of breathing, mantra chanting in meditation, the disclosure of awesome mysteries, special lighting and sound effects, programmed response to incense, or intoxicating drugs. The same results can be obtained in contemporary psychiatric treatment by electric shock treatments and even by purposely lowering a patient's blood sugar level with insulin injections.

Before I talk about exactly how some of the techniques are applied, I want to point out that hypnosis and conversion tactics are two distinctly different things, and that conversion techniques are far more powerful. However, the two are often mixed, with results that are equally powerful.

How Revivalist Preachers Work

If you'd like to see a revivalist preacher at work, there are probably several in your city. Go to the church or tent early and sit in the rear, about three-quarters of the way back. Most likely, repetitive music will be played while the people come in for the service. A repetitive beat, ideally ranging from 45 to 72 beats per minute (a rhythm close to the beat of a human heart), is very hypnotic and can generate an eyes-open altered state of consciousness in a high percentage of people. Once you are in an alpha state, you are at least 25 times as suggestible as you would be in full beta consciousness. The music is probably the same for every service, or incorporates the same beat, and many of the people will go into an altered state almost immediately upon entering the sanctuary. Subconsciously, they recall their state of mind from previous services and respond according to the post-hypnotic programming.

Watch the people waiting for the service to begin. Many will exhibit external signs of trance: body relaxation and slightly dilated eyes. Often they begin swaying back and forth with their hands in the air while sitting in their chairs. Next, the assistant pastor will come out. He usually speaks with a "voice roll."

The Voice Roll Technique

A "voice roll" is a patterned, paced style used by hypnotists when inducing a trance. It is also used by many lawyers (several of the most famous are highly trained hypnotists) when they desire to entrench a point firmly in the minds of the jurors. A voice roll can sound as if the speaker were talking to the beat of a metronome, or it may sound as though he were emphasizing every word in a monotonous, patterned style. The words will usually be delivered at the rate of 35 to 60 beats per minute, maximizing the hypnotic effect.

Now the assistant pastor begins the "build-up" process. He induces an altered state of consciousness and/or begins to generate the excitement and the expectations of the audience. Next, a group of young women in "sweet and pure" chiffon dresses might come out to sing a song. Gospel songs are great for building excitement and involvement. In the middle of the song, one of the girls might be "smitten by the Spirit" and fall down or react as if possessed by the Holy Spirit. This effectively increases the intense atmosphere in the room. At this point, hypnosis and conversion tactics are being mixed. As a result, the audience's attention is now totally focused upon the communication, while the environment becomes more exciting or tense.

Right about this time, when an eyes-open mass-induced alpha mental level has been achieved, attendants will usually pass the collection plate. In the background, a 45-beat-per-minute voice roll from the assistant preacher might exhort, "Give to God . . . Give to God . . . Give to God . . ." And the audience does give. God may not get the money, but his already wealthy representative will.

Next, the fire-and-brimstone preacher will come out. He induces fear and increases the tension by talking about the Devil, going to hell, or the forthcoming Armageddon. In the last such rally I attended, the preacher talked about the blood that would soon be running out of every faucet in the land. He was also obsessed with a "bloody ax of God," which attendees had seen hanging above the pulpit the previous week. I have no doubt that some people saw it: the power of suggestion given to a group of people in hypnosis ensures that at least 10 to 25 percent would see whatever he suggested they see.

In most revivalist gatherings, "testifying" or "witnessing" usually follows the fear-based sermon. People from the audience come up on stage and relate their stories. "I was crippled, and now I can walk!" "I had arthritis, and now it's gone!" It is a type of psychological manipulation that works. After listening to numerous case histories of miraculous healings, the average guy in the audience with a minor problem is sure he can be healed. The room is charged with fear, guilt, intense excitement, and expectations.

Now those who want to be healed are frequently lined up around the edge of the room, or they are told to come down to the front. The preacher might touch them on the head firmly and scream, "Be healed!" This releases the psychic energy, and for many, catharsis results. Individuals might cry, fall down, or even go into spasms. If catharsis is effected, they stand a chance of being healed. In catharsis, the brain slate is temporarily wiped clean, and the new suggestion is accepted.

For some, the healing may be permanent. For many, it will last four days to a week (a week is, incidentally, how long a hypnotic suggestion given to a somnambulistic subject will usually last). Even if the healing doesn't last, if they come back every week, the power of suggestion may continually override the problem. Or sometimes, sadly, it can mask a physical problem which could prove to be very detrimental to the individual in the long run.

I'm not saying that legitimate healings do not take place. They do. Maybe the individual was ready to let go of the negativity that caused the problem in the first place; maybe it was the work of God. Yet I contend that these healings can be explained with existing knowledge of brain/mind function.

The techniques and staging will vary from church to church. Many use "speaking in tongues" to generate catharsis in some, while the spectacle creates intense excitement in the observers.

The use of hypnotic and conversion techniques by religions is sophisticated, and professionals are ensuring that they become ever more effective. A man in Los Angeles is designing, building, and reworking many churches around the county. He tells ministers what they need and how to use it. This man's track record indicates that the congregation and the monetary income will double if the minister follows his instructions. He admits that about 80 percent of his efforts result from the sound system and lighting.

Powerful sound and the proper use of lighting are of primary importance in inducing an altered state of consciousness; I've been using them for years in my own seminars. However, my participants are fully aware of the process and of what they can expect as a result of their participation.

Conversion Techniques

Cults and human-potential training companies are always looking for new converts. To attain them, many use conversion tactics, which must be effective within a short space of time—usually a weekend, but in some cases as quickly as a single day. The following are the six primary techniques used to generate the conversion.

Conversion tactic 1. The meetings or training takes place in an area where participants are cut off from the outside world: a private home, a remote or rural setting, or a hotel ballroom, where the participants are allowed only limited bathroom usage. In human-potential trainings, the controllers will give a lengthy talk about the importance of "keeping agreements" in life. The participants are told, "If you don't keep your agreements, your life will never work." Generally, this is good advice, but the controllers are subverting a positive human value for selfish purposes. The participants vow to themselves and their trainer that they will keep their agreements. Anyone who doesn't concur will be intimidated into agreement or forced to leave the training.

The next step is to get the participants to agree to complete the training, thus assuring a high percentage of conversions for the organization. They will usually have to agree not to take drugs, smoke, and sometimes not to eat, or they are given such a short meal break that it creates tension. One of the real reasons for the agreements is to alter internal chemistry, which generates anxiety and hopefully causes at least a slight malfunction of the nervous system, which in turn increases the conversion potential.

Before the gathering is complete, the agreement's manipulation will be used to ensure that the new converts go out and find new participants. They are intimidated into agreeing to bring in at least two potential converts. Since the importance of keeping agreements is so high on their priority list, the converts will twist the arms of everyone they know, attempting to talk them into attending the free introductory session offered at a future date by the training organization. The new converts are zealots. The inside term for merchandising one of the largest and most successful human-potential trainings is, "Sell it by zealot!" At least a million people are graduates and a good percentage have been left with a mental activation button that ensures their future loyalty and assistance if the guru figure or organization calls. Think about the potential political implications of hundreds of thousands of zealots programmed to campaign for their guru.

Be wary of an organization of this type that offers follow-up sessions after the seminar. Follow-up sessions might be weekly meetings or inexpensive seminars given on a regular basis, which the organization will attempt to talk you into taking. These regularly scheduled events are used to maintain control. As the early Christian revivalists found, long-term control is dependent upon a good follow-up system.

Conversion tactic 2. A schedule is maintained that causes physical and mental fatigue. This is primarily accomplished by long hours in which the participants are given no opportunity for relaxation or reflection.

Conversion tactic 3. Techniques are used to increase the tension in the room or environment.

Conversion tactic 4. Uncertainty. One of the most effective ways of creating uncertainty is to subject the participants to the fear of being "put on the spot" or encountered by the trainers who play upon guilt feelings or convince the participants to verbally relate their innermost secrets in front of the others. Activities that emphasize the removal of masks is another powerful ploy. One of the most successful human-potential seminars forces the participants to stand on a stage in front of the entire audience while being verbally attacked by the trainers. A public poll showed that the most fearful of all situations is to speak to an audience. It ranked above window washing outside the eighty-fifth floor of an office building. So you can imagine the fear and tension this situation generates within the seminar participants who have agreed to complete the training.

Many faint, but most cope with the stress by mentally going away. They go into an alpha state, which automatically opens them to being 25 to 200 times more suggestible. And another loop of the downward spiral into conversion is successfully effected.

Conversion tactic 5. The introduction of jargon—new terms that have meaning only to the insiders who have participated in the training. Vicious language is also frequently used to purposely make participants uncomfortable.

Conversion tactic 6. There is no humor in the communications until the participants are converted. At that point, merrymaking and humor are highly desirable as symbols of the new joy the participants have supposedly found.

I'm not saying that good does not result from participation in such gatherings. But it is important for people to know what has happened and to be aware that continual involvement may not be in their best interest.

Over the years, I've conducted professional seminars to teach people to be hypnotists, trainers, and counselors. Many of those who conduct human-potential training and rallies (from the training companies who use the tactics I've just described) come to me and say, "I know what I'm doing works, but I don't know why." After I've shown them how and why, many have gotten out of the business or have decided to approach it differently or in a much more loving and supportive manner.

Many of these trainers have become personal friends, and it scares us all to have experienced the power of one person with a microphone and a room full of people. Add a little charisma, and you can count on a high percentage of conversion. The sad truth is that a high percentage of people seem to want to become true believers and give away their power.

Cult gatherings or human-potential trainings are an ideal environment to observe firsthand what is technically called the *Stockholm syndrome*. This is a situation in which those who are intimidated, controlled, or made to suffer begin to love, admire, and even sometimes sexually desire their controllers or captors.

But let me inject a word of warning here: if you think you can attend such gatherings and not be affected, you are probably wrong. A perfect example is the case of a woman who went to Haiti on a Guggenheim Fellowship to study Haitian Voodoo. In her report, she related how the music eventually induced uncontrollable bodily movement and an altered state of consciousness. Although she understood the process and thought herself above it, when she began to feel herself become vulnerable to the music, she attempted to fight it and turned away. (Anger or resistance almost always assures conversion.) A few moments later, she was possessed by the music and began dancing in a trance around the Voodoo meeting house. A brain phase had been induced by the music and excitement, and she awoke feeling reborn.

The only hope of attending such gatherings without being affected is to be the Buddha and allow no positive or negative emotions to surface. Few people are capable of such detachment.

I once attended est (Erhard Seminar Training). The training is no longer offered; a later incarnation of the seminar was called The Forum.

My goal in attending was to be an observer—to be Buddha throughout the process, which took place in a Phoenix hotel ballroom with 200 people attending. I remained detached until late afternoon of the final day, when a doctor stood up and accused the est trainer of using brainwashing tactics. The incensed trainer argued back, using ridiculous Zen riddles to try to intimidate the doctor.

After forty-five minutes of ranting, the trainer began using the other participants against the protesting doctor, who was speaking the truth. That did it. I stood up, snapped a karate kick at an est staffer, and took a spare microphone out of his hands (the kick was to distract and did not inflict pain). Then I verbally went after the trainer. He responded by yelling for his people to call the police. Both the doctor and I walked out of the training room as the police arrived.

I'm probably still listed in the est computers as someone who doesn't keep agreements.

Before leaving the six conversion tactics, I should mention military boot camp. The Marine Corps talks about breaking men down before rebuilding them as new men—as Marines. That is exactly what they do, the same way a cult breaks its people down and rebuilds them as happy flower sellers on your local street corner.

Every one of the six conversion techniques are used in boot camp. Considering the needs of the military, I'm not making a judgment as to whether this is good or bad. But as a simple fact, these men are brainwashed. Those who won't submit must be discharged or will spend much of their time in the brig.

Decognition Process

Once the initial conversion is effected, cults, armed services, and similar groups cannot have cynicism among their members. Members must respond to commands and do as they are told; otherwise they are dangerous to the organizational control. This is normally accomplished as a three-step *decognition process*.

Step 1: alertness reduction. The controllers cause the nervous system to malfunction, making it difficult to distinguish between fantasy and reality. This can be accomplished in several ways. Poor diet is one; watch out for brownies and Kool-Aid. The sugar throws the nervous system off. More subtle is the "spiritual diet" used by many cults. They eat only vegetables and fruits; without the grounding of grains, nuts, seeds, dairy products, fish or meat, an individual becomes mentally spacy. Inadequate sleep is another primary way to reduce alertness, especially when combined with long hours of work or intense physical activity. Being bombarded with intense and unique experiences achieves the same result.

Step 2: programmed confusion. You are mentally assaulted while your alertness is being reduced, as in step 1. This is accomplished with a deluge of new information, lectures, discussion groups, encounters, or one-to-one processing, which usually amounts to the controller bombarding the individual with questions. During this phase of decognition, reality and illusion often merge, and perverted logic is likely to be accepted.

Step 3: thought stopping. Techniques are used to cause the mind to go flat. Altered state of consciousness techniques initially induce calmness by giving the mind something simple to deal with that focuses awareness. Continued use brings on a feeling of elation and eventually hallucination. The result is the reduction of thought and eventually, if used long enough, the cessation of all thought and withdrawal from everyone and everything except that which the controllers direct. The mental takeover is then complete.

It is important to be aware that when members or participants are instructed to use thought-stopping techniques, they are told that they will benefit by so doing: they will become better soldiers or attain enlightenment.

There are three primary techniques used for thought stopping:

- **Marching.** The thump, thump, thump beat generates self-hypnosis and thus greater susceptibility to suggestion. In the early stages of his rise to power, Adolf Hitler used marching demonstrations and the resulting excitement as a mass conversion technique for those attending his rallies and in the decognition phase for his soldiers.

- **Meditation.** If you spend ninety minutes or more a day in meditation, after a few weeks there is high probability that you will not return to full beta consciousness. You will remain in a fixed state of alpha for as long as you continue to meditate. I'm not saying this is bad; if you do it yourself, it may be very beneficial. But know that you are causing your mind to go flat. I've worked with meditators on an EEG machine, and the results are conclusive: the more you meditate, the flatter your mind becomes, until—eventually and especially if used to excess or in combination with decognition—all thought ceases. Some spiritual groups call this nirvana, but this is just another manipulation. The mental state is simply a predictable physiological result. If heaven on earth is nonthinking and noninvolvement, I really question why we are here.

- **Chanting.** Often chanting in meditation. Speaking in tongues could also be included in this category.

All three thought stopping techniques produce an altered state of consciousness. This may be desirable if you are controlling the process, for you also control the input. I personally use at least one self-hypnosis programming session every day, and I know how beneficial it is for me. But you need to know that if you use these techniques to the degree of remaining continually in alpha, although you'll be very mellow, you'll also be more suggestible.

True Believers and Mass Movements

Before ending this section, I want to talk about the people who are most susceptible to conversion and joining mass movements. I am convinced that at least a third of the population are what philosopher Eric Hoffer calls "true believers." They are joiners and followers—people who want to give away their power. They look for answers, meaning, and enlightenment outside themselves.

Hoffer's 1951 book *The True Believer* is a classic work on mass movements. He says, "True believers are not intent on bolstering and advancing a cherished self, but are those craving to be rid of an unwanted self. They are followers, not because of a desire for self-advancement, but because it can satisfy their passion for self-renunciation!" Hoffer also says that true believers "are eternally incomplete and eternally insecure."

In my years of conducting seminar trainings, I have constantly run into true believers. All I can do is advise them to seek the true Self within, where meaningful personal answers will be found. I teach that the basics of spirituality are self-responsibility (karma) and the attainment of self-actualization (being compassionate, while also accepting others without judgment, expectations, blame or attempting to control.) But most of the true believers just tell me that I'm not spiritual and go looking for someone who will give them the dogma and structure they desire.

Never underestimate the potential danger of these people. They can easily be molded into fanatics who will gladly work and die for their holy cause. It is a substitute for their lost faith in themselves and offers a substitute for individual hope. Hitler's Brown Shirts were true believers. The Moral Majority and similar groups are made up of true believers. All cults are composed of true believers. You'll find them in politics, churches, businesses, and social cause groups. They are the fanatics in these organizations.

Mass movements will usually have a charismatic leader. The followers want to convert others to their way of living or impose a new way of life—if necessary, by legislating laws forcing others to their view, as evidenced by the activities of the Moral Majority. This means enforcement by guns or punishment, which is the bottom line in law enforcement.

A common hatred, enemy, or devil is essential to the success of a mass movement. Hitler's devil was the Jews. The born-again Christians have Satan himself, but that isn't enough. They've added the New Age and all who oppose their integration of church and politics, as evidenced in the political reelection campaigns against those who oppose their views. In revolutions, the devil is usually the ruling power or aristocracy. Some human-potential movements are far too clever to ask their graduates to join anything, thus labeling themselves a cult—but upon close examination, you'll find that their devil is everyone who hasn't taken their training. There are mass movements without devils, but they seldom attain major status.

True believers are mentally unbalanced or insecure people, or those without hope or friends. People don't look for allies when they love, but they do when they hate or become obsessed with a cause. And those who desire a new life and a new order feel the old ways must be eliminated before the new order can be built.

Persuasion Techniques

Persuasion isn't technically brainwashing, but it is a manipulation of the human mind without the manipulated party being aware what caused his opinion shift. I can only introduce you to a few of the many techniques in use today, but the basis of persuasion is always to access your right brain.

The left half of your brain is analytical and rational. The right half is creative and imaginative. That is overly simplified, but it makes my point. The idea is to distract the left brain and keep it busy. Ideally, the persuader generates an eyes-open altered state of consciousness, causing you to shift from beta awareness into alpha—a shift that can be measured on an EEG machine.

First, let me give you an example of distracting the left brain. Politicians use these powerful techniques all the time; lawyers use many variations which, I've been told, they call "tightening the noose."

Assume for a moment that you are watching a politician give a speech. First, he might generate what is called a yes set. These are statements that will cause most listeners to agree; they might even unknowingly nod their heads in agreement. Next come the truisms. These are usually facts that could be debated but, once the politician has his audience agreeing, the odds are in the politician's favor that the audience won't stop to think for themselves, thus continuing to agree. Last comes the suggestion. This is what the politician wants you to do and, since you've been agreeing all along, you could be persuaded to accept the suggestion. In the sample political speech below, you'll find that the first three statements are the yes set, the next three are truisms, and the last is the suggestion.

Ladies and gentlemen: are you angry about high food prices? Are you tired of astronomical gas prices? Are you sick of out-of-control inflation? Well, you know the Other Party allowed 18 percent inflation last year; you know crime has increased 50 percent nationwide in the last 12 months, and you know your paycheck hardly covers your expenses anymore. Well, the answer to resolving these problems is to elect me, John Jones, to the US Senate.

You've heard it all before. But you might also watch for what are called embedded commands. As an example: On key words, the speaker makes a gesture with his left hand, which research has shown is more apt to access your right brain. Today's media-oriented politicians and spellbinders are often carefully trained by a whole new breed of specialists, who are using every trick in the book, both old and new, to manipulate you into accepting their candidate.

The concepts and techniques of neurolinguistics are so heavily protected that I found out the hard way that to even talk about them publicly or in print results in threatened legal action. Yet neurolinguistic training is readily available to anyone willing to devote the time and pay the price. It is some of the most subtle and powerful manipulation I've ever seen. A good friend who recently attended a two-week seminar on neurolinguistics found that many of those she talked to during the breaks were government people.

Another slippery form of manipulation is called an *interspersal technique.* The idea is to say one thing with words but plant a subconscious impression of something else in the minds of the listeners and viewers.

As an example, assume you are watching a television commentator make the following statement: "Senator Johnson is assisting local authorities to clear up the stupid mistakes of the companies contributing to the nuclear waste problems." It sounds like a statement of fact, but if the speaker emphasizes the right word, and especially if he makes the proper hand gestures on the key words, you could be left with the subconscious impression that Senator Johnson is stupid. That was the subliminal goal of the statement, but the speaker cannot be sued for libel.

Persuasion techniques are also frequently used on a much smaller scale with just as much effectiveness. The insurance salesman knows his pitch is likely to be more effective if he can get you to visualize something in your mind. This is right-brain communication. For instance, he might pause in his conversation, look slowly around your living room and say, "Can you just imagine this beautiful home burning to the ground?" Of course you can! It is one of your unconscious fears, and in forcing you to visualize it, he is more likely to manipulate you into signing his insurance policy.

The cults operating in airports use what I call shock and confusion techniques to distract the left brain and communicate directly with the right brain. While waiting for a plane, I once watched one operator for over an hour. He had a technique of almost jumping in front of someone. Initially, his voice was loud, then dropped as he made his pitch to take a book and contribute money to the cause. Usually, when people are shocked, they immediately withdraw. In this case, they were shocked by the strange appearance, sudden materialization, and loud voice of the devotee. In other words, the people went into an alpha state for security because they didn't want to confront the reality before them. In alpha, they were highly suggestible, so they responded to the suggestion of taking the book; the moment they took the book, they felt guilty and responded to the second suggestion: give money. We are all conditioned so that if someone gives us something, we have to give them something in return.

While watching this hustler, I was close enough to notice that many of the people he stopped exhibited an outward sign of alpha: their eyes dilated.

Subliminal Programming

Subliminals are hidden suggestions, perceived only by your subconscious mind. They can be audio suggestions, hidden behind music, or visual suggestions airbrushed or cleverly incorporated into a picture or design, or words or images flashed on a screen so fast that you don't consciously see them.

Some subliminal programming tapes offer verbal suggestions recorded at a low volume. I question the efficacy of this technique: if subliminals are not perceptible, they cannot be effective, and subliminals recorded below the audible threshold are therefore useless. The oldest audio subliminal technique uses a voice that follows the volume of the music, so subliminals are impossible to detect without a parametric equalizer. But this technique is patented, and when I wanted to develop my own line of subliminal audio programs, negotiations with the patent holder proved to be unsatisfactory. My attorney obtained copies of the patents, which I gave to talented Hollywood sound engineers, asking them to create a new technique. They found a way to psychoacoustically modify and synthesize the suggestions so that they are projected in the same chord and frequency as the music, thus giving them the effect of being part of the music. But we found that in using this technique, there is no way to reduce various frequencies to detect the subliminals. In other words, although the suggestions are being heard by the subconscious mind, they cannot be monitored with even the most sophisticated equipment.

If we were able to come up with this technique as easily as we did, I can only imagine how sophisticated the technology has become with government or advertising funding. I shudder to think about the propaganda and commercial manipulation that we are exposed to on a daily basis. There is simply no way to know what is behind the music you hear. It may even be possible to hide a second voice behind the voice to which you are listening.

The series of books by Wilson Bryan Key, PhD, on subliminals in advertising and political campaigns well documents the misuse in many areas, especially printed advertising in newspapers, magazines, and posters.

The big question about subliminals is: do they work? Based upon the response from those who have used my tapes, the answer is yes. Subliminal suggestions behind the music in department stores can be advising customers not to shoplift. An East Coast department store chain reported a 37 percent reduction in thefts in the first nine months of testing this form of suggestion.

A 1984 article in the technical newsletter *Brain-Mind Bulletin* states that as much as 99 percent of our cognitive activity may be nonconscious, according to the director of the Laboratory for Cognitive Psychophysiology at the University of Illinois. The lengthy report ends with the statement, "These findings support the use of subliminal approaches such as taped suggestions for weight loss and the therapeutic use of hypnosis and Neuro-Linguistic programming."

Mass Misuse

I could relate many stories that support subliminal programming, but I'd rather use my time to make you aware of even more subtle uses of such programming.

I have personally experienced sitting in a Los Angeles auditorium with over 10,000 people who were gathered to listen to a charismatic figure. Twenty minutes after entering the auditorium, I became aware that I was going in and out of an altered state. Those accompanying me experienced the same thing. Since it is our business, we were aware of what was happening, but those around us were not. By careful observation, what appeared to be spontaneous demonstrations were, in fact, artful manipulations. The only way I could figure how the eyes-open trance had been induced was that a 6- to 7-cycle-per-second vibration was being piped into the room behind the air conditioner sound. That vibration generates alpha, which would render the audience highly susceptible. Ten to 25 percent of the population is capable of a somnambulistic trance level. For these people, the suggestions of the speaker could potentially be accepted as commands.

Vibrato

Vibrato is the tremulous effect imparted in some vocal or instrumental music, and the cycle-per-second range causes people to go into an altered state of consciousness. At one period of English history, singers whose voices contained pronounced vibrato were not allowed to perform publicly, because listeners would go into an altered state and have fantasies that were often sexual in nature. People who attend opera or enjoy listening to singers like Mario Lanza are familiar with this altered state induced by the performers.

ELFs

Now let's carry this awareness a little farther. There are also inaudible ELFs (extra-low-frequency waves). These are electromagnetic in nature. One of the primary uses of ELFs is to communicate with our submarines. Dr. Andrija Puharich, a highly respected researcher, in an attempt to warn US officials about Russian use of ELFs, set up an experiment. Volunteers were wired so their brain waves could be measured on an EEG. They were then sealed in a metal room that could not be penetrated by a normal signal.

Puharich then beamed ELF waves at the volunteers. ELFs go right through the earth and right through metal walls. Those inside couldn't know if the signal was or was not being sent. And Puharich watched the reactions on the technical equipment: Thirty percent of those inside the room were taken over by the ELF signal in six to ten seconds.

When I say "taken over," I mean their behavior followed the changes anticipated at very precise frequencies. Waves below 6 cycles per second caused the subjects to become emotionally upset, and even disrupted bodily functions. At 8.2 cycles, they felt high—as though they had been in masterful meditation, learned over a period of years. Eleven to 11.3 cycles induced waves of depressed agitation, which could lead to riotous behavior.

The Neurophone

Dr. Patrick Flanagan is a personal friend. In the early 1960s, as a teenager, Pat was listed as one of the top scientists in the world by *Life* magazine. Among his many inventions was a device he called the Neurophone—an electronic instrument that can successfully program suggestions directly through contact with the skin. When he attempted to patent the device, the government demanded that he prove it worked. When he did, the National Security Agency confiscated the Neurophone. It took Pat two years of legal battle to get his invention back.

In using the device, you don't hear or see a thing; it is applied to the skin, which Pat claims is the source of special senses. The skin contains more sensors for heat, touch, pain, vibration, and electrical fields than any other part of the human anatomy.

In one of his tests, Pat conducted two identical seminars for a military audience, one seminar one night and one the next night, because the room was not large enough to accommodate all the attendees at one time. When the first group proved to be very cool and unwilling to respond, Patrick spent the next day making a special tape to play at the second seminar. The tape instructed the audience to be extremely warm and responsive and for their hands to become tingly. The tape was played through the Neurophone, which was connected to a wire he placed along the ceiling of the room.

There were no speakers, so no sound could be heard, yet the message was successfully transmitted from that wire directly into the brains of the audience. They were warm and receptive, their hands tingled, and they responded according to programming in other ways that Pat doesn't want publicly discussed.

The Medium for Takeover

The more we find out about how human beings work, the more we learn to control human beings. What scares me most is that the medium for takeover is already in place! The television set in your living room and bedroom may be doing a lot more than just entertaining you.

Before I continue, let me point out something else about an altered state of consciousness. When you go into an altered state, you transfer into right brain, which results in the internal release of brain opiates: enkephalins and beta-endorphins, which are chemically almost identical to opium. In other words, it feels good, and you want to experience more.

Tests by researcher Herbert Krugman showed that while viewers were watching TV, right-brain activity outnumbered left-brain activity by a ratio of two to one. Put more simply, the viewers were in an altered state more often than not. They were getting their beta-endorphin fix.

To measure attention spans, psychophysiologist Thomas Mulholland of the Veterans Hospital in Bedford, Massachusetts, attached young viewers to an EEG machine that was wired to shut the TV set off whenever the children's brains produced a majority of alpha waves. Although the children were told to concentrate, only a few could keep the set on for more than thirty seconds.

Most viewers are already hypnotized. To deepen the trance is easy. One simple way is to place one blank black frame for every 32 frames in the film that is being projected. This creates a 45-beat-per-minute pulsation, perceived only by the subconscious mind—the ideal pace to generate deep hypnosis.

The commercials or suggestions presented following this alpha-inducing broadcast are much more likely to be accepted by the viewer. The high percentage of the viewing audience that naturally attains a somnambulistic depth could very well accept the suggestions as commands—as long as the commands did not ask the viewer to do something contrary to his morals, religion, or self-preservation.

The medium for takeover is here. By the age of sixteen, children have spent 10,000 to 15,000 hours watching television—more time than they spend in school. In the average home, the TV set is on for 6 hours and 44 minutes per day.

A research project by Jacob Jacoby, a Purdue University psychologist, found that of 2,700 people tested, 90 percent misunderstood even such simple viewing fare as commercials or a TV series they watched regularly. Only minutes after watching a show, the typical viewer missed 23 to 36 percent of the questions about what they had just seen. Maybe this is because they were going in and out of trance. When in a deep trance, you must be instructed to remember; otherwise you forget consciously, while your subconscious mind remembers everything.

The Tip of the Iceberg

I have just touched the tip of the iceberg. When you start to combine subliminal messages behind the music, subliminal visuals projected on the screen, hypnotically produced visual effects, and sustained musical beats at a trance-inducing pace, you are talking conversion: brainwashing. Every hour that you spend watching TV you become more conditioned. In case you thought there was a law against any of these things, guess again. There isn't. There are a lot of powerful people out there who probably have plans for you.

Selected Bibliography

Camellion, Richard. *Behavior Modification: The Art of Mind Murdering*. Boulder, Colo.: Paladin, 1978.

Cialdini, Robert B., PhD. *Influence: The Psychology of Persuasion*. Rev. ed. New York: Harper Business, 2006.

Conway, Flo, and Jim Siegelman. *Holy Terror: The Fundamentalist War on America's Freedoms in Religion, Politics, and Our Private Lives*. New York: Delta, 1982.

———. *Snapping: America's Epidemic of Sudden Personality Change*. New York: Delta, 1978.

Hoffer, Eric. *The True Believer*. San Francisco: Harper & Row, 1951.

McCoy, Duke. *How to Organize and Manage Your Own Religion Cult*. Mason, Mo.: Loompanics, 1980.

McRae, Ron. *Mind Wars: The True Story of Government Research into the Military Potential of Psychic Weapons*. New York: St. Martin's, 1984.

Sargant, William. *The Battle for the Mind: How Evangelists, Psychiatrists, Politicians, and Medicine Men Can Change Your Beliefs and Behaviour*. London: Heinemann, 1957.

Waugh, Charles G., and Martin H. Greenberg, eds. *Cults: An Anthology of Secret Societies, Sects, and the Supernatural.* New York: Beaufort, 1983.

See also all books on subliminal control by Wilson Bryan Key.

Cause and Effect

For many years I've conducted metaphysical research, counseled people, and conducted psychic, reincarnation and human-potential seminars. As a result of my work, I'm convinced that everything of importance in your life is predestined—of karmic origin. That doesn't mean you don't have free will, and it doesn't mean you can't change aspects of your life. But basically, you're living the life you were born to live, in the body you designed for karmic growth.

In my book *Unseen Influences*, I have described seventeen primary influences. From a higher perspective, all the influences have been invoked to fulfill the need of karmic balance and learning. Many can be included under the following four categories:

1. Past-life programming.
2. Spirit possession syndrome.
3. Your spiritual home is "elsewhere" (star people, wanderers, walk-ins).
4. Psychometric and/or telepathic sensitivity.

Telepathic Sensitivity

The following letter from Susan is typical of my daily mail. It represents the kind of problem psychologists, psychiatrists, and counselors usually cannot explain or resolve through conventional therapeutic techniques. Susan attended a seminar retreat and later wrote me about her problem.

Dear Richard,

I am writing to you because I know of no where else to turn, and after attending the Lake Arrowhead retreat, I have faith in your advice. Now, I wish I had brought it up when we were all together in the mountains, but I was too embarrassed. You see, many years ago I was involved in an on-again, off-again relationship with a man I came to care for very much. Eventually, we went our separate ways, and I haven't heard from him since. After our parting, I did quite well, except every three or four months when I'd start remembering, and be unable to get him out of my thoughts. The feelings would be overwhelming and very distressing.

In time, I stumbled upon a method which helped. When the feelings would begin to overwhelm me, I would put everything down in a letter to him, then seal and address the envelope and put it away. Within a week, the feelings would pass, and I would burn the letter. After five years, it's the only thing that seems to help.

Lately, everything has become more intense. The memories now linger on between the episodes—becoming more disturbing by the month. My life is busy, and I'm concentrating on developing my talents and creating the life I desire. But no matter what I do, the thoughts keep coming back with regularity. I'm desperate to find peace and put it all behind me.

Your books have helped me understand why I'm here, and I know I have to move forward, take risks, and keep my mind open. Is there anything else you can tell me that could explain or help me to resolve this situation?

Here is my response.

Dear Susan,

Aside from psychological considerations best accessed by a local counselor, there are several psychic considerations. All would result from you being highly empathic (telepathically sensitive), and could manifest as any of six factors: (1) You and your ex-lover may have near identical brain waves. As an example, you may both be alpha-sevens, and your shared history has resulted in an on-going telepathic link. Subconsciously, you're always in communication, but it's only when you've received a several month buildup of awareness that it begins to bleed through. Once you relieve the pressure by responding, you're open to begin receiving again. (2) He may be purposely sending telepathic messages to you. (3) He's simply thinking about you, and you're telepathically picking it up. (4) You're occasionally contacting him "out-of-body" on the other side while sleeping at night, and the contact lingers. (5) Dreams, resulting from unconscious longing, are reinforcing the union. (6) He has died, is earthbound, and is coming to you, generating the effects you're experiencing.

After another letter exchange with Susan, I asked a psychic to investigate with automatic writing. She contacted her spirit guide, who then made contact with Gwendolyn, a woman in Spirit who knew Susan in the lifetime responsible for the problem. The psychic described Gwendolyn as a petite woman, blonde, dressed in nineteenth-century attire. This is what she had to say:

Ireland: Susan's name was Franklin. He was a dashing, daring prize fighter within the confines of our prison camp. The guards couldn't break him so they made money from him, by putting him out on the circuit. We remained in the prison camp, and were later shipped to Australia, losing touch with him.

Eventually, Franklin too was sent to Australia, a paralyzed, broken man. He just happened to come to our small camp, men carrying him. I had always looked up to him, and in Australia, I helped care for him many years—as if he were the child I never bore. He loved me in his way, but it was not the love of a woman and man. As his physical condition deteriorated, he called out to others, sisters, past loves, people we did not know.

In this life as Susan, he no longer wishes to fight, but he retains a desperate longing for loving connections that he feels were denied him in that life. As Susan, when the relationship in question ended, she subconsciously used her empathic abilities to retain the connection. Unfulfilled passions karmically carry over as a powerful force. In this case, because she has a natural telepathic ability, she manifested a connection as Dick described in his response. She "feeds" on the connection, then reaches a saturation point and reacts, trapping herself, much as she was trapped in the past life.

Susan should focus her meditations upon vividly visualizing this connection being cut. She can imagine it in many forms: chopping the connection, burning it, dissolving it. It is time for her to find peace, so she can prepare for a new love that awaits.

In Love, Gwendolyn

In another case of telepathic sensitivity, a young man named Daniel told how his life took a downward spiral after he received a raise and moved to a new apartment. "From day one, it seemed like a dark cloud descended upon my life. I moved in over the weekend, excited about living in such a nice place. The complex had a beautiful pool and lots of single girls in residence. But by Monday morning, I awakened extremely depressed. It got worse and worse. On long weekends, with friends up in Big Bear, I'd be fine. But as soon as I got home, I became depressed. I even saw a psychologist. After three visits, she advised I get a thorough physical. Nothing. To make a long story short, several months ago, I threw a party. A buddy I work with brought a psychic—a woman who does those 900 number phone readings. She had to leave, because the vibes in the apartment were so bad."

"Did the psychic say anything else?" I asked.

"She wanted to know if someone had been murdered there. It scared me. I asked my neighbors about the previous residents. I learned the couple was evicted. Everyone thought he was a drug addict. Neighbors called the police several times because of their terrible fights. The psychic explained that the psychometric vibrations of the previous residents are still there—permeating the walls and appliances. I'm evidently very empathic, and I was drawing in the negativity, thinking it was my own creation."

"Did you move?"

"You bet. And my state of mind returned to normal within a week."

Past-Life Programming

Since all is karmic, all problems, restrictions, obsessions, and fear-based emotions, unless traceable to this life, are the result of past-life programming (and even then, past lives probably set the current life events into motion). Assuming karma is the universal basis of reality, even if you're from elsewhere, you've chosen to come to earth and interact with the rest of us for karmic reasons.

The following examples are from individual regressions I've conducted at our retreats and from group regressions in which individual participants have shared their experiences.

The purpose of past-life regression, when used as a therapeutic tool, is to find the cause of the current effect, and ideally to accelerate the needed learning and heal the soul.

Jonathan was in his late thirties and in business for himself in San Diego, California. "No matter what I do, I can't seem to grow beyond the level of success I've already attained. It's not that I'm not successful, it's just that my growth seems blocked. I try, but my efforts beyond this 'line in the sand' invariably fail. Why?"

In a back-to-the-cause group regression, Jonathan found his own answer: "I was living in Amsterdam in the early 1900s, and owned a carriage business. Things were going well until I decided to expand. The result was disastrous. Do you think I'm subconsciously holding myself back because I fear the same thing happening again?"

"Probably," I said. "But it's false-fear karma, one of the easiest kinds of karma to resolve. Often just knowing the cause is enough to release the effect. Wisdom erases karma. In your daily meditations or programming sessions, I'd advise you to include this mantra: 'I know the cause, release the effect, and succeed beyond my grandest dreams.' Then visualize the success goal you desire as an already accomplished fact. Repeat the mantra over and over. Within a few months, I bet you'll raise your level of success."

Lauren was in her early thirties and unable to conceive a child. "My husband and I have been to two fertility clinics, spent a lot of money, and have had no results. It's so frustrating," she said.

In a retreat group regression, she found out why: "In my last life, I committed suicide. I was only fifteen, and my parents were devastated by my act. This time around, I have to learn about the value of human life and begin to balance the suffering my loss caused my parents. But my husband, Keith, is also affected, and when you took me up into Higher Self, I obtained a karmic overview. It seems that Keith relished the taking of enemies' lives in World War II. Fighting for your country is one thing, but finding joy in killing creates karmic debits. Again, it's a lesson regarding the value of human life."

"Did you receive any advice when I asked how you could invoke the Law of Grace?" I asked.

"By giving mercy and grace, I'll open the door to receive the same in return. I'm going to meditate on it."

Group-Focus Regression

In a group-focus regression, one person (the subject) lies on the floor, their head cradled in a volunteer's lap. The other retreat participants (healers) sit around the subject, laying their hands upon the subject's body. I ask the subject to explain the nature of their problem. Then I induce everyone into a meditative state of consciousness, using a chakra process to open and charge the aura, and mentally chakra-link the subject to the healers. Once done, I direct the subject back to the cause of the problem.

Next, I guide a regression, and everyone perceives impressions of the subject's past life. The healers draw down Universal healing energy and expand it until they can focus the force in their hands, which become very hot. At the point of maximum energy, I ask them to release their energy into the subject. Healing suggestions and a self-forgiveness process follow. The experience is incredibly powerful for all involved; the results for the subject are usually profound.

Example: Mary, thirty-eight, attended a retreat with twenty-two other people from all over the country. On a crisp fall evening, we all gathered around a blazing fire-place in the meeting room. Mary lay on the floor, her head cradled in Marsha's lap, with six people sitting on each side and two more at her feet. Those who were not touching Mary sat in yoga positions nearby, notebooks in their lap.

"Can you tell us what is troubling you, Mary?" I asked.

Voice breaking, she said, "Three months ago, my hus-band, Mark, left me for another woman. We were married twenty-one years. As a result of all the conflict, I haven't paid enough attention to my gift shop, which is now in seri-ous financial trouble. I have two children, one boy, one girl—teenagers. They live with me, and they seem to be taking their anger out on me. Last week, my daughter said, 'Maybe if you'd been a better wife, Daddy wouldn't be liv-ing with Karen.'" Mary began to cry.

Relaxation, chakra links, and induction completed, I directed Mary to go back to the cause of her current prob-lems. By going back to the cause, the subject can attain awareness in the current life or past lives. Mary was the only one directed to speak. The healers were to observe through the chakra-link mental method, which allowed them to perceive and feel what Mary was experiencing.

"What do you see, and what are you doing?" I asked.

For a few moments Mary had difficulty forming words. "The only impression I'm receiving is of my spirit guide,

Verona, sitting beside me, talking to me. She's as vivid and real as you all were before I closed my eyes for this session."

This was unusual—more apt to occur in a Higher Self session than under these conditions. I assumed it was the power of the group energy transference. "What is Verona saying?" I asked.

"Mark and I have been together many, many times, and we'd have to look at most of those incarnations to fully understand our current relationship. Let me listen for a moment, and then if it's OK with Verona, I'll just repeat her words."

Silence.

"It's OK, wait." Silence.

When Mary began to speak, her words were halting, without emotion. "You have outgrown Mark. You came together again in hopes of balancing your shared karma. The more you became interested in metaphysics, the more he pulled away. For the last six years, you have not been happy; you know that, Mary. You will soon have a karmic opportunity to embrace another. You will love him and he you, and he will support your growth."

"Was Mary's divorce predestined?" I asked.

"There is always hope that one will evolve beyond what is destined."

"But was the divorce predestined?"

"As you would understand it, yes."

"I'm missing something?" I asked.

"There was planned karmic growth between Mary and Mark. Think of it as balancing conflicting energy. There was a little growth on Mark's part, much growth on Mary's part. Resolving karma often takes many incarnations."

"Why is there so much karmic conflict between them?"

"It is a long story that begins in medieval times. Mary and Mark were incarnated in the gender roles they chose today. Mary and other women of her English village were branded as witches. Mark was the cruel accuser. In the next life, Mary balanced the score in Wales as a male renegade who raped and stabbed a female Mark. They have reincarnated eleven times since. The last five lives have shown considerable progress. There is no longer physical abuse, and they have come to love as well as hate each other."

"What about Mary's failing business?"

"She has free will in this regard, and by focusing her energy upon the gift shop, she can save it. Subconsciously, she allowed the crisis to develop because Mark helped her establish the business. She would rather be doing something new, something without attached memories. Now is the time to follow her heart."

After Mary was awakened, several of the healers talked about Verona. "She had long blond hair, didn't she?" asked Sharon.

"Yes," Mary said, smiling.

"And she was wearing a toga with a braided-white tie," said Daniel. Mary nodded.

"How many others visualized Verona this way?" I asked.

Of the nine who chakra-linked with Mary, seven put up their hands. One of the remaining two said, "I saw the toga, but I thought her hair was light brown."

Wanderers and Walk-Ins

Since I began professionally researching metaphysics in the early seventies, a high percentage of the people I've worked with have told me that they felt they didn't belong here. Something within their psyches was telling them that their true home was elsewhere.

In those early days, I also had several regressive hypnosis meetings with those I called "light people" in my early books—people who experienced past lives as nonphysical light beings. At the time, it seemed to me that they had somehow flunked that advanced level of experience and had been sent back to earth to experience material reality once again before being allowed to return home.

Today I'm not sure this was an accurate assumption. Considering other people's investigations, it seems more likely that the light people incarnated to serve a planet in need of help.

My friend Brad Steiger once wrote a series of Star People books. The series was based upon extensive research and seems to generally agree with a new study published as *From Elsewhere*, by Scott Mandelker, PhD.

According to Mandelker's research (his PhD dissertation), those who feel that the earth is an alien place usually don't connect their deep sense of being different with the possibility of a nonearthly origin. They are born of earthly parents to fulfill an earthly purpose, and they fall into two categories: "wanderers" and "walk-ins."

Wanderers are souls who have incarnated from a more evolved civilization, with memories of their identity and true origin blocked—just as memories of past lives are blocked until investigated with metaphysical techniques. Wanderers have volunteered for the purpose of serving humanity. This service may be subtle, or the wanderer may be destined to become a major influence.

Once born, wanderers are as ordinary as everyone else, so it takes a real metaphysical effort for them to realize their true identity. According to Mandelker, if they don't remember, they can easily become entangled in all the earthly snares and never fulfill their plans. In *From Elsewhere*, he describes many characteristics of wanderers, including these:

1. As children, they were thought of as being odd.
2. They are genuinely kind, gentle, peaceful, nonaggressive people.
3. They are not very interested in money or material things.
4. They have a hard time recognizing manipulation and trickery.
5. They cherish great ideals.
6. They have a strong interest in metaphysics and/or UFOs.
7. They've always felt alienated.

Walk-ins are souls who participated in a "soul transfer" with a human being who wished to depart from the physical world without dying and without incurring additional karma. The departing soul often feels overpowered and incapable of handling life. An agreement is reached while the person is sleeping and out-of-body on the other side. Then the walk-in steps in with the departing soul's memory banks intact. Once the transfer is made, the walk-in doesn't remember what has occurred, but is intuitively driven to clean up the problems of the departing soul. After this task is completed, the walk-in is free to pursue their own humanitarian service agenda.

A walk-in's entrance is usually signaled by someone finally getting their life together. The transfer can take place after an accident or near-death experience, but a trauma isn't necessary for the transference to occur. Sometimes the walk-in appears different to those closest to them. After the old problems are resolved, the walk-in sometimes divorces, drops old friends, and begins a new career.

Before sharing some current wanderer statistics, I need to provide a little backstory. In past seminars, when I directed a "Parallel Life Search," almost everyone participating was able to tap into a parallel life (described in detail in my book, *Past Lives, Future Loves*).

In the early eighties, when Ruth Montgomery began writing about walk-ins, she and I were working together on some seminars. I included a "Walk-In Search" to see if any participants were walk-ins. Although everyone wanted to be a walk-in, only one person in 100 perceived that they actually were one, and it was a boring session for everyone else. I feel it is important to note that nobody made up being a walk-in. Statistically, according to Ruth's research, the percentage made sense when compared to the number she said were walking in.

A few years ago, I conducted a Psychic Prophecy Seminar in six cities: Dallas, Houston, Philadelphia, New York, Riverside, and Los Angeles. The average attendance was 100 participants per city. In every city, almost 50 percent of the participants perceived themselves as "wanderers." It didn't vary from city to city. At a couple of seminars, no one perceived themselves as walk-ins, while in others, we'd find two or three out of 100: the same statistics we had obtained fourteen years before.

Etherealization?

In *Past Lives, Future Loves*, I reported on a session with trance psychic Kingdon Brown that may relate to the wanderers being here to help:

There is the impression that this planet was indeed seeded somehow. That the souls here in physical bodies were brought here, and that we are under some incubation, or gestation period that has been going on. The reason this is becoming evident is that there is a life-giving continuity here that does not exist elsewhere in the universe in quite this way. The intelligences are still monitoring our progress. I see . . . I'm now getting this directly. It's like a veil or blinders . . . like the Bible says, through a glass darkly. This veil is being removed very carefully to see if we can make this leap, or advancement, without falling backwards into disintegration once again, as has happened so many times in history. This is what transcendence means. We become something else. There is an experiment going on with this planet, and the intelligences that are observing it are not taking part directly, for it happens automatically at a certain point. They are observing to see if this time we can accept evolutionary knowledge and true change. There is something here about the relationship of all your past, present, and future physical explorations transpiring in a constant now, and that you will all have to make this change at once. Everybody has to make it. An instantaneous thing, without falling back again into a dark age, or a point where all is hidden once again.

Later in the session, Kingdon seems to expand upon this concept:

Well, I'll have to say this the way it comes to me, but it seems incredible to me. I can't censor it, because that would defeat the purpose of this. We are moving towards a point of "etherealization" . . . Ah, we don't really have a word for it in English. We are attempting to move to a place where we do not exist in physical bodies, yet we exist in an etheric way in which all is totally clear to us . . . as to what has transpired and why we then exist. I'm also receiving with this . . . this is the reason it's so difficult for me to comprehend . . . that at some point when we have reached this degree of evolution, a decision will then be made as to whether or not it will be necessary to continue this planet. It will either be entirely destroyed . . . or something. What I'm seeing visually is that all of these souls that have been interconnected here and interrelated are fragmenting out the way a dandelion sends seeds out, and they are going out everywhere. I'm being told that this is why this is an incubating place, where all this care has been placed through centuries of bringing human beings past the state of experimentation into the point of self-creating. But they are self-perpetuating in an etheric way, or through a spiritual essence, an astral essence. We create spiritually . . . spiritual propagation . . . ah, there is love. Love is a propagating of the spiritual nature. We will no longer recreate in the way we do now, for we no longer need these bodies, but are in light bodies, and we propagate in a vibration that we call love.

Maybe the wanderers are here to help us make this transition. For them, it may be a matter of returning home.

Spirit Possession Syndrome

Psychologist Edith Fiore combines psychotherapy with past-life regression and the treatment of spirit possession syndrome (SPS)—problems caused by the spirits of the deceased interfering with the living. Soon after Dr. Fiore began incorporating past-life investigation into her therapy, she recognized that over half her clients exhibited signs of spirit interference. The more she worked with patients suffering from SPS and learned to recognize the signs and symptoms, the more she became convinced that at some time in their life, nearly everyone is influenced by nonphysical beings to some degree, and for varying periods.

Spirit interference ranges from subtle influence to attachment to full possession of a living human by a discarnate—the surviving consciousness of a deceased individual. In other words, according to Dr. Bill Baldwin, "The entity becomes a parasite in the mind of the host."

One of the most frequently asked questions in seminars is about how a spirit becomes earthbound after death. My response: By lowering their level of awareness, their vibrational rate, while living. This could result from an addiction, such as a drug, alcohol, or sexual dependency. After death the earthly desire remains, and in a futile attempt to fulfill their craving, the newly deceased soul clings to living souls that are similarly afflicted. Long-term anger lowers our vibrational rate, as does extreme fear, jealousy, greed, resentment, remorse, or guilt, or the ruthless quest for personal power. Love manifesting as an obsessive need to remain with the lover can keep a soul earthbound.

In some cases, an ongoing spirit attachment can manifest in lifetime after lifetime, as explained in "Debra Wakefield," the opening chapter of my book *Predestined Love*. In such cases, the attaching entity is angry or resentful about some past injustice and seeks retribution.

One of my first contacts with an earthbound entity was in a house I bought on an old gold claim in the Arizona mountains. Even my teenage son could perceive the cold, undesirable presence. In time, I set up a session to contact the discarnate—a miner who had worked the area. His partner had hit him in the side with a shovel, and he died slowly over an extended period of time, filled with anger. Although he had been dead for nearly 100 years, his side still hurt, and he didn't understand why no one talked to him anymore.

Through spirit contact with those who loved him in life, I was able to send him to the light. After the session, I learned that my new neighbors had occasionally seen manifestations of an old miner in their kitchen.

Mahatma Gandhi, when shot by an assassin, is said to have verbally forgiven his murderer as he died. He knew not to create a karmic tie or to allow blame, anger, or hatred to keep him earthbound.

A Case History

Kevin wasn't aware that a whole nest of entities had attached to him during a period he was drinking himself into a nightly stupor. It was only after four weeks in a detox center that he realized that, although sober, he was experiencing desires that made no logical sense to him, especially homosexual urges. An understanding therapist explored the SPS potential.

Once Kevin was in an altered state, the therapist drew out a male named Christopher. Through lengthy dialogue, the therapist learned that Christopher was the elected voice of a dozen other souls, all of whom had been alcoholics in life, and several had been gay. This group of parasites was angry at Kevin for denying them their contact high, and when they couldn't get him to drink, they began mentally prodding him to have sex with a man. The therapist successfully banished the spirits. Today, Kevin doesn't drink and is happily married.

The Vibrational Rate

Increasing your level of awareness raises your vibrational rate, which is the unconscious quest of everyone on this planet. Raising your rate can also help to avoid the problems connected with spirit interference. Although this cannot ensure that you won't experience SPS, it is difficult for an entity of a lesser vibration to influence an entity of a higher vibration. It is also good insurance to establish communication with your own guides and Masters in meditation.

Think of the spiritual planes as a ladder down a well. Each rung of the ladder is on a different level—a different vibrational rate. The bottom rungs are damp, dark, cold, and of low vibration. As you climb the ladder, the atmosphere becomes lighter and warmer, and the rate of vibration increases. Your goal is to get to the top and climb out onto the celestial plane (nirvana, the God level, the seventh level, or satori 3). Spiritually, you want to get there. To do so, you must raise your vibrational rate, and this can be achieved more rapidly in the physical body than in spirit.

The lower levels—the lower astral planes—are undesirable and similar to the classic concept of purgatory. Like spirit interference, hauntings and apparitions are caused by confused entities who have trapped themselves on the lower astral plane. They have the ability to rise above their situation, even on the other side, but it often takes hundreds of earth years for them to realize they are free to go to the light. In time, they listen to the advice of more advanced souls who are always willing to help. On numerous occasions, while regressing someone into a past life, I have had a subject find themselves on the lower astral. The reaction is always the same and is usually described as confusing, dark, and fearful. The fact that these subjects have been reborn on the earth plane shows that they worked their way out of the situation.

At the time of death, you will cross over, leaving the physical body, and again become the spiritual being you actually are. Your vibrational rate at this time will dictate your level on the other side. If there are seven upper astral levels and you have the vibrational rate for the third level, this is as high as you'll be able to go. You could not withstand the more intense vibrations on the fourth through seventh levels.

What determines your vibrational rate? Your thoughts, words, and deeds on the earth plane will determine your level of awareness, which determines your vibrational rate. Since you have to think something before you speak or act, it really goes back to your thoughts.

You were born with a vibrational rate you established in the past. The way you live your life will determine whether you raise or lower the rate during this incarnation. If you changed your way of thinking, speaking, and acting today, your vibrational rate would begin to change tomorrow.

Love, positive thoughts, and helping others would raise your level of awareness. Hate, negative thoughts, and hurting others mentally or physically would lower your level of awareness.

Metaphysical teachers often say that it is possible to advance fifteen to twenty lifetimes during this life you're now living, if you choose to do so.

Part 4

THE MULTIMILLIONAIRE MINDSET

This was a manual with six audio programs offered in Dick Sutphen's magazines. I'm including this because it shows the research he would go through to bring out the best information he could to his audience. It also contains personal stories he used as examples.

The Multimillionaire Mindset

What is a millionaire? Some people say you have to have a million dollars in the bank to qualify as a millionaire. Others say you need a million dollars' worth of assets. A third definition says you need to gross a million dollars in profits a year. When you get down to it, a million dollars isn't all that much in today's society. So on the audio programming MP3s that accompany this training, I use the term "multimillionaire."

Whatever your definition, this seminar is about ultrasuccess and financial freedom. Personally, I define *ultrasuccess* as financial wealth and career satisfaction combined with personal freedom, a loving relationship, and a self-actualized perspective on life.

Establish your own vision, and don't settle for anything less. You'll never succeed beyond the size of your vision.

Most of you have already read or heard what I'm going to say. But maybe you weren't ready for it at the time. Maybe you couldn't picture yourself ultrasuccessful, but now you're ready to hear, absorb, and act on the awareness.

If you want to be ultrasuccessful and you aren't, your mind isn't set for millionaire status. Your mind is a biocomputer. Your inner beliefs manifest your outer reality.

"As within, so without." Beliefs generate your thoughts and emotions, which in turn create your experiences. Back in the fifties, Maxwell Maltz wrote *Psycho-Cybernetics*—the book that first exposed these ideas to the general public. As a plastic surgeon, Maltz was frustrated by the fact that he could operate on unattractive or disfigured patients and make them beautiful, but even when they looked in the mirror, they still saw themselves as they did before the plastic surgery.

As an adjunct to his work as a surgeon, Maltz began to work with mind programming to change his patient's beliefs. And it worked. He obtained amazing results. His research was one of my primary inspirations in experimenting with hypnosis tapes in the mid-seventies. Hypnosis tapes, sleep programming tapes, subliminal tapes all do one thing and one thing only: they program new beliefs. Change your beliefs, and you change your life.

To become ultrasuccessful, you need a multimillion-aire mindset or prosuccess beliefs. I'm not talking about easy-to-spot surface beliefs like religion and politics. I'm talking about deep-seated restrictive beliefs programmed by parents, church and society, and if you believe in rein-carnation, beliefs programmed by past lives. These beliefs are working against you.

Let me explain something important about beliefs. There is a Universal law that says: You cannot become what you resent. If your beliefs express resentment, they are automatically blocking your success. As a related example, if you pull up to a stoplight beside a man driving a brand-new Rolls-Royce, and you experience a surge of resentment, it's an expression of your belief about wealthy people. Since you can't become what you resent, your belief is blocking you.

Here's another Universal law: you will always live up to your self-image. If you think rich people are snobs, you're certainly not going to allow yourself to be a snob, so you automatically block success. I realize this sounds simplistic, but please understand that it accurately reflects *what is*. This kind of belief block can assure that you'll never become ultrasuccessful.

If you think rich people are lucky, that doesn't work any better: since you're not rich, you obviously aren't lucky. It is another self-created belief block.

If you want to attain and retain wealth, you need to eliminate your belief blocks and prepare your mind for a multimillionaire mindset.

A financial magazine recently ran a lengthy article on state lottery winners—people who were not programmed with a multimillionaire mindset. The article reported how winning the lottery made most people miserable. They lost their friends, messed up their marriages and family relationships, and in the majority of cases, if the payoff was immediate, quickly lost the money—probably as a subconscious attempt to regain normalcy in their lives.

To attain and retain abundance, you need ultrasuccessful beliefs. And you cannot will things such as love or hope or belief. There are five human wills: the will to power, pleasure, meaning, self-actualization, and death. You can't will a multimillionaire mindset. You have to eliminate your belief blocks, and then you have to program the new mindset.

Sure—all your past decisions and commitments have created your current reality, but those decisions and commitments were generated by your beliefs. Many of these have not served you. But if you can accept the responsibility for your life up to now, you have the power to create an ultrasuccessful reality. Wisdom erases karma.

High Achiever Personality Profile

The following points in this profile are the combined results of two studies and my own observations in conducting seminars on this subject for decades.

Statistics show that high achievers:

1. Are self-confident.
2. Are impatient and excessive about their personal and professional pursuits.
3. Are committed to their work to the extent of being workaholics.
4. Want, need, and demand to be in control.
5. Have strong likes and dislikes.
6. Are introverted as opposed to extraverted.
7. More concerned with being respected than being liked.
8. Find the process of attaining their goals much more joyful than the actual accomplishment.
9. Are predictable and reliable high achievers, who always act to secure their future.
10. Need to learn to delegate.

If you don't fulfill all these profile points, that doesn't mean you can't learn to become successful. YOU CAN!

Six Traits of Millionaires

1. **Clarity of intent.** You must know what you want if you expect to get it. Merely getting rich isn't a valid goal; it's about knowing what you want to do to get rich. The Oracle of Delphi itself couldn't step down and tell you what you should want. You have to decide, or nothing will change. Do you know what you want to do that will make you a multimillionaire? Start by pretending you're Dorothy in the Wizard of Oz, and all you have to do is click your magic red slippers to have what you want—no logical restrictions. What would you wish to be if you could have any wish you wanted?

What do you want out of life? Not what *should* you want, or what someone else thinks you should want. What do you want? Maybe you think your real wants are greedy, so you disguise them. Or you feel they are irresponsible or unrealistic, so you won't admit to them—even to yourself.

What do you want to do? Don't put excuses between you and doing it. Excuses are automatic blocks.

Here's another way to explore what you want to do: Take a look at your role models, going all the way back to high school. Who are the people you admired? List them. Then check and see if there is a common trait.

When I did this, I found several common traits in my role models, some that pushed me forward and some that held me back. Without realizing it, I had subconsciously become a composite of my role models' common traits without ever having consciously thought about it. The good news is, you're always free to choose new role models . . . ones that support your current desires.

2. They enjoy what they do. To become a multimillionaire, you have to love to do something. For most people, work is something they do to maintain their lifestyle. But millionaires seldom feel as if they're working. Their work is their play. They enjoy what they do. If you don't love the vehicle you'll use to become a millionaire, you'd better find a way to change your attitude about your work, or find a new career.

Most of the millionaires I know consider vacations work. Their career is their play. Exactly the opposite of 99 percent of the population.

3. They concentrate their powers. Millionaires tend to concentrate all their power on the vehicle they use to make money. They don't try to do many things. They don't go off on tangents, because when you do, you're distracted from the area of your greatest potential.

When you focus all your power on one area, you quickly learn from your mistakes, and the more you learn, the more your productivity increases. In learning all there is to learn about your area of expertise, you lower your chance of failure.

4. They have an emotional purpose. You need an emotional purpose to fulfill a large vision, because an emotional purpose will drive you forward through the good times and the bad.

For example, the desire to be one of the best in your field is an emotional purpose. The desire to send your kids to Harvard is an emotional purpose. To flaunt your success to all the people who used to laugh at you is an emotional purpose.

Once I was conducting a seminar with Richard Bach, author of the best-selling book *Jonathan Livingston Seagull*. We were sitting in a hotel room talking about success and what drove us. We decided we both were still reacting to our fourth-grade classmates. I explained, "I was always the last kid they picked to be on the basketball team."

"You too?" Richard replied. "They never wanted me either."

Let's look at practical purposes. If you simply want to pay the mortgage more easily or afford a nicer car, those are not emotional purposes: they're practical purposes. Instead of fulfilling such practical goals, you'll probably tend to reduce your desires the moment the going gets tough.

One thing is sure: no matter what their emotional purpose, millionaires have excessive ego drives behind that purpose, and they're relentlessly driven to be winners.

5. They have a positive self-image. Many people feel that perceiving yourself as a winner is the most powerful success force of all, because your outer life is a projection of your inner beliefs. As within, so without.

Self-image results from what you do. The more you act in ways that make you proud of yourself, the better your self-image.

Stop doing anything that lowers your self-image. Maybe you lend out your car when you don't really want to. Not being willing to stand up and say no lowers your self-esteem. Maybe you commit to a diet, but you quickly give up on it. A lack of willpower lowers your self-esteem. When you do things that lower self-image, you harm yourself far more than you realize, because you will never allow yourself to have what you don't feel worthy of attaining.

Exercise: close your eyes and meditate for a few moments upon what you feel worthy of.

6. **They make decisions and act.** Millionaires are willing to take risks. It goes with the territory. You learn to analyze and evaluate, then you make a decision and act upon it. To be highly successful, you'll have to evaluate and act over and over again.

The Six Primary Blocks That Keep You from Acting

Until you recognize these blocks, you'll continue to feel overwhelmed and unable to forge ahead.

1. **Lack of clarity.** We've already discussed this. Without clarity you cannot act to manifest money.

2. **Fear of change.** People find security in their insecurity, and they resist change. But change is inevitable, no matter how much you resist it. So the idea is to make changes on your own, directing them so they work for, not against you.

All resistance goes back to the one and only problem in the Universe—*fear.* In this case, it is a matter of fear of being unable to control the outcome, which might also be viewed as fear of the unknown.

Over the years in which I've conducted seminars, I've heard some amazing reasons why people fear change. They usually don't know the reason consciously, but the reasons come out in the altered state sessions and processing. One woman never allowed herself to succeed beyond the level of her father's success, although she was certainly capable of doing so. She came to realize that if she allowed herself to outdo her father, he would be hurt, and she loved him too much to allow that to happen.

A major block for many people is the loss of friends. If you become a millionaire, you stand a good chance of losing a lot of your friends, because your success will reflect their failure. That's *what is*. You'll have to find new friends who are comfortable in abundance.

How do you deal with the fear of change? First, accept *what is*. Things will change, and maybe for the worse. So force yourself to act. Ask yourself, "What do I have to lose?" Know that if you refuse to act, there's no possibility of controlling the situation. But if you act, there is a good chance of controlling the situation.

3. Waiting for someone or something to step in and save you. It isn't going to happen. It's up to you to make it happen.

Maybe you're waiting for financing. That's not a valid excuse. Get creative. Think like an entrepreneur, not like a businessman. The best way I can communicate this concept is to provide a few of my own publishing case histories:

First case history. In the mid-sixties I wanted to get into publishing. I didn't have any money, but I knew there was a market for my books. I'd created a two-volume set of high-priced books for the professional advertising market. My solution was to convince a local printer that the books would be successful. He agreed to print the books for me when he wasn't busy on other jobs, and he would keep them in his warehouse. I could buy them from him as I needed them, and I agreed to buy them all within one year. He charged me an extra 50 cents per book (an additional 20 percent in those days) for gambling along with me. The result: the books sold by the thousands. There was a need both in this country and in fifteen foreign countries, especially Japan, for just this type of material. Fifteen additional titles sold well for nearly twenty years.

Second case history. Following a divorce, I had little spare capital, but I wanted to publish a huge encyclopedia for the professional art/advertising market. At this time I was living in a different city, and I came up with a different solution. I contacted art supply stores all over the world and explained that if they would sign a contract to buy a certain number of my books and agree to pay me within thirty days of delivery, I would buy ads in many trade publications listing their store as the primary dealer in their city. It worked fantastically. I then took the signed contracts to a printer, who gladly agreed to extend credit. It might have been easier with a bank, but I have a typical entrepreneur's aversion to banks.

Third case history. I wrote and assembled *The Mad Old Ads* as a general market book on the history of advertising and the need for laws to control advertising practices. I published 3,000 copies for the love of it, thinking I could sell the book to the same people who were buying my other advertising books. Review copies were sent out to all major newspapers and magazines.

The result was an explosion of good reviews. For starters, *Newsweek* devoted over a full page to the book, and the *Chicago Tribune* gave it a half page. At the time, there was no sophisticated nationwide system for ordering books, and bookstores didn't know how to get in touch with me to order mine. So I quickly sent copies to major publishers, offering to sell the rights. Both McGraw Hill and Doubleday said yes. I went with McGraw Hill. The book went through several editions, and rights were sold to an English publisher. In the end, the book did even better in Europe.

Although I didn't go with Doubleday, my contact with editor Julie Coopersmith at that company proved to be of great value years later. I had just finished writing *You Were Born Again to Be Together* when Julie decided to leave Doubleday to become a full-time literary agent. She placed my book with Simon & Schuster Pocket Books in 1976, and it has remained in print for forty-four years.

Fourth case history. In 1977 I published a book about my seminars written by my friend Alan Weisman. At the time, Alan was having a hard time finding enough writing assignments to live comfortably. I offered him $1500 in advance money if he'd write the book. (He was living in the Arizona mountains in the 1970s, and his house payment was $25 a month.) He happily agreed on the condition that I couldn't change anything: the book had to be seen through his eyes. Once it was published, we sold copies through mail order and at the seminars. We also sent copies to New York mass-market paperback publishers offering to sell the rights. Both Avon and Pocket Books responded with offers. I went with Pocket Books. They paid a good advance and soon the book, *We Immortals*, was available in bookstores and paperback racks throughout the country. It was also an ad for my seminars.

Fifth case history. The Master of Life Manual was a little book expressing my personal philosophy. To demonstrate the ideas, it related verbal exchanges from my Bushido Training. The title proved to be a life-changing book for many. It was also a superb way to merchandise the Bushido Training seminar. The initial idea was to mail the book to everyone on my mailing list (35,000 buyers or seminar attendees at that time). Along with each book, I sent a contribution envelope and a note that said, "If you feel this book improves your life and you are willing to support this free distribution, please send us $2 or more." Within a few weeks I received far more money than if I'd sold the book for $2. Thousands of people ordered more copies to give to friends. The initial print run was 50,000 and it was soon out of print. I quickly reprinted. The book went on to sell 155,000 copies, and after reading it, people wanted to attend the Bushido Training.

Promoting a seminar with a book worked even better with *Sedona: Psychic Energy Vortexes*. The book created an interest in my Sedona Psychic Seminar for decades.

I could relate many more of my own publishing stories, but I think you get the idea. There is always a way to put together a deal and make it work. Do it yourself. And now let's get back to the six primary blocks that keep you from acting.

4. Lack of aliveness or motivation. Aliveness is real enjoyment in doing what you do. It's the excitement and exhilaration that makes you feel glad to be alive and feel the joy, stimulation, and pleasure that makes life worth living. The best way I've found to generate aliveness and motivation is to do what you really want to do. What you want appears to be the best option in life, because life appears to be set up for you to get what you want, if you dare to want it. So, when you're making choices, choose what you want most, not what appears to make the most sense.

To overcome lack of aliveness and to motivate yourself, get involved in what really interests you. You must have strength-producing activity in your life, or you will become depressed. Your mind will never allow life to become too boring and mundane without doing something to make it more interesting. The problem is, your mind might generate fights with your mate (when you're in mental pain, at least you know you're alive) or an illness (kidney stones would give you something to talk about), or an accident (endangering your life will create a lot of aliveness). Act and make your life interesting before your mind does it for you.

5. Overwhelm. This is when you feel that what you want involves so much time, effort, money, or sacrifice (or any combination of these factors) that you can't bring yourself to act. Maybe you're overwhelmed because you already have too many irons in the fire—too many projects, and you're busy full-time trying to keep it all together. In other words, you don't have enough energy or focus left to do what has to be done.

So what do you do about it? Accept that you can only do so much. You can only stretch yourself so far. Then decide what is most important. Ask yourself, "What really matters?" Once you've come up with the answer, eliminate everything that isn't crucial to your goal. *Decide, then act intelligently.*

In the process, explore all your excuses. Why are you so busy you don't have time for anything? Maybe you're hiding. Maybe you need to learn to delegate. If you're so busy you don't have a moment of spare time, maybe you need to reduce your lifestyle, which in return would reduce the pressure while you're gearing up to do what will really work.

If you're overwhelmed by the size of your goal, break it down into steps and handle them one at a time, starting with the most important. Focus your full attention upon what is most important. Finalize it; then, and only then, move on to the next step.

6. **Doubting your ability to accomplish your goal.** This is another block to acting that is not valid. Success comes to those who recognize a need, figure out how to fill it, and then proceed intelligently, never giving up. Although these people often feel insecure and inadequate, that doesn't stop them.

There is always the possibility of failure. Most people have failed along the way, but winners get back up, find a new dream, and begin pursuing it. If you fell off a bicycle ten times trying to learn to ride it, you needed those ten failures to achieve your success. In reality, you needed ten minor successes before you could attain your real success in mastering the bicycle.

The Chinese have a theory about success and failure. They say that no matter what you attempt to accomplish, whether you succeeded or fail, it is more important that you at least act in an attempt to succeed. They believe if you take action, in the long run, you'll succeed no matter how many times you fail. Not taking action is a much bigger disgrace than failing.

I personally try a lot of things. I launch a lot of ideas, and many of them fail, but some of them succeed. I figure if I win two out of five times, I'm usually well ahead of the game.

Seven Basic Tips

1. **Sell what you do at least three times.** Bob Rosefsky has been a close friend since the 1970s. A radio and TV financial commentator, he has also written many books on money, including a title used as the basis of a PBS-TV series. Because of some important financial advice Bob provided, I'm probably a lot more successful than I might have been. At an early point in my career, he said, "Always find a way to sell what you do at least three times." It was advice I took seriously.

My current career started when I began to investigate regressive hypnosis and offered private hypnosis sessions as a sideline to my creative advertising/art studio business. Soon I was writing about my experiences and sold a book to Simon & Schuster Pocket Books. The books created interest in my work, and I created hypnosis tapes to offer to those who wrote to me. The books and tapes led to conducting seminars. That's three times.

By continuing to grasp each new opportunity, I continued to compound my core offerings. In creating a magalog (magazine-catalog), I kept my readers informed and interested, and it allowed me to present related offers, including other people's books and tapes. Then there were all the spin-off opportunities. I needed New Age music as background music for my tapes. Originally I licensed the rights to use other musicians. I soon began to offer a line of New Age music, sold through mail order, distributors, and directly to stores, and also licensed its use to others.

If I write a book today, I also release it as a digital book, and I sell the rights to many foreign countries. The contents of these books create interest in my work, and I offer my own seminars based on my latest communications.

If selling something three times sounds unique to a business like mine, it isn't. I used to do the same thing as an art director, an advertising/art publisher, and a studio owner.

2. Whatever you're going to offer, **you must perfect your ability in that area.** In other words, you have to become very good at what you do. When you have mental experience of mastery, you project it to others.

I've met a lot of people who desire the benefits of mastery, but they aren't willing to pay the price in effort and sacrifice. If you're halfway realistic about your goal, you can accomplish it as long as you're willing to pay the price. There's always a price, and you need to know it ahead of time.

3. **Structure what you're going to love around your personality.** I'm very much a loner who needs to be insulated by an organization so I can work uninterrupted on my own and with my creative team. I don't take phone calls or have meetings other than with advertising people and my own staff.

I love the creative side of the business, and to do it, I have to delegate most contracts and a lot of management to others. To me, the joy and challenge is always the creative process—the marketing manipulations. I attended Art Center School in Los Angeles and started out as an advertising agency art director. I loved the work and won 150 major advertising awards in the process. I'm not telling you this to brag, but to make a point: I never really changed professions: *I just added to what I was already doing.*

Much of my time is spent coming up with advertising and promotions ideas for books, CDs or MP3s, and seminars. Then I find ways to make them work by writing hot copy, designing ads and packaging. I usually write all the ad and promo copy first. That's the fun part. Then it's easy for me to create the product, seminar, or service to fit what is marketable.

So look at two things:

How can you add to what you do now? You're already very good at something. The man who invented video games worked summers as a carnival game barker. Later, as an electrical video engineer, he combined people's love of games with the latest video technology. He added to what he knew.

What kind of business fits your personality? If you're a natural entrepreneur, you don't belong working as a part of a corporate team. If you're comfortable on a corporate team, you probably would not make a good entrepreneur.

4. Pick something to be passionate about that has the potential of being economically viable. You have to be responsible to your goals by investigating the market potential for your idea, or service, or product. In other words, if you want to be a huge success as a past-life therapist in a Mississippi town with a population of 20,000, it might be quite a challenge. Thoroughly investigate the potential of your idea.

5. Recognize any destructive patterns from your past. They must be considered in planning your future. Furthermore, don't do what you're not good at. If I were to do my own website management, I would be mediocre at this task. It's much better to delegate these jobs to those who do them well.

6. Set goals or establish strong general directions, and then monitor your accomplishments. Today, I prefer the idea of a strong general direction. I know what I want to accomplish, but I've learned that the Universe can present opportunities that might be missed if I were to focus solely upon the goal.

For example, my strong general direction is to communicate metaphysical and self-actualized awareness to as many people as possible. If I limited my goals to books or audio sales, I might bypass the potentials offered by the Internet, radio, TV or other media.

In establishing my goals and directions, as a matter of course, I ask myself, "Does the goal in any way manipulate or forcibly infringe upon the rights of other human beings?" If it does, I consider it a bad goal.

Another good question to ask yourself is, "When I accomplish the goal, will it give me more peace of mind?" If it will, it is probably a good goal.

7. **Know the truth about yourself.** The incoming sensory data we receive is often influenced by our own fears, anxieties or desires. To be effective in business, you must be willing to acknowledge the truth about *what is.* Unless you do, you cannot respond appropriately.

How to Get Ideas

Background yourself so that you are totally familiar with the subject you desire to explore. You need a full understanding of the field and its needs and potentials, plus the beliefs accepted by others in the field. You must learn everything that's already known if you expect to be able to tell the difference between an intelligent idea and a cliché.

Request the idea from your Higher Mind or Spirit. Be very clear about what you want and the purpose of your idea.

Write it down. The purpose is important, because there may be many ways to fulfill it. Then think about what you want often, especially as you go to sleep. Ask your own guides and Masters to assist you in coming up with an idea. Keep a pen and paper nearby to record your dreams immediately upon awakening.

This technique has worked for me again and again. Sometimes the answer comes as a symbolic dream, sometimes as words echoing in my head as I awaken. On several occasions, the dreams have resolved major problems.

Positioning

How can you possibly stand out in today's extremely crowded marketplace? The place to start looking for answers is *positioning.* Positioning seeks to find a unique position for your product or service—one that will make an impression on your potential customers.

Many of the examples I'll be quoting are from the series of books on this subject by Al Ries and Jack Trout, such as *Positioning: The Battle for Your Mind.* They first established the concept, which today is used by most advertising and marketing professionals. In providing examples, I'll primarily use national names everyone can relate to.

1. **Find a position to be first in.** Examples: Kleenex, Hertz, Xerox, and Apple. In metaphysical communications, Edgar Cayce was the first nationally recognized psychic. Although he is no longer with us, his communications and the Association of Research and Enlightenment, the orga-

nization he built around his work, are more active than ever. Another example: I created and marketed the first hypnosis tapes.

To quote Ries and Trout, "You must create a position in the prospect's mind—a position that takes into consideration not only your own strengths and weaknesses, but those of your competitors as well."

According to Harvard psychologist George Miller, the average human mind cannot deal with more than seven units at a time. In any given category, from brand names to metaphysical leaders, rarely can anyone name more than seven. You want to be one of those seven names in your given category. The higher up, the more likely you are to be purchased.

2. If you can't be the first in your field, can you position yourself against your competitors? The first step is to analyze your competitor's positions. Avis positioned itself against Hertz with "We're number 2, so we try harder" campaign. 7-Up positioned itself against Coke and Pepsi with its Uncola campaign, starting in 1968.

Many people, products, and services produced great advertising and promotion but still failed, because they were in a no-win position. If a position is already filled—if another company is already established and successful—it is very difficult to get people to switch loyalties. The first rule of positioning says, to win and establish a place in people's minds, you can't compete head-on against those who have already established a strong position in your field. You can go around, under, over, but never head-to-head.

3. If you can't position yourself as first or against, can you find a point of difference for your product or service? When cars were big and flashy along came Volkswagen with a short, fat and ugly automobile. When Merrill Company wanted to get into the cold remedy field, they didn't take on Contac, which was then at the top. Instead they produced Nyquil, "the nighttime cold medicine"—a position they now own.

Several years ago, one company brought out a line of subliminal tapes that offered millions of subliminal suggestions on each tape—tapes supposedly so superior that they were sold for $35 each. This was a real point of difference, and for a while, a lot of people purchased them, because the claim sounded logical. But in reality, millions of subliminal suggestions on one tape would be nothing but white noise.

4. If the first three positions aren't available, can you reposition your competition? This probably means that you will have to overturn an old idea. Repositioning is undercutting an existing concept, product, or individual. Conflict can build your reputation overnight. (But be careful: it can also get you sued.)

You have to say something about your competitor that causes the prospective buyer to change his mind, not only about you and your product or service, but about your competition and his product or service.

Examples: Scope repositioned Listerine, then the mouthwash leader, with its "Medicine Breath" campaign. Burger King repositioned McDonald's with its "Have it your way" campaign.

In your positioning, the biggest mistake you can make is to attempt to be all things to all people. Find one specific concept, and run with it.

Some key questions:

If you're already in business, what position can you claim? What position do you want to claim?

If you're considering a new business, what position do you want to claim?

To establish your desired position, do you have to out-gun someone else?

Can you afford to do it?

Do you and your personality match the position you desire to claim?

Do not launch your effort without a well-researched positioning paper.

Image Making

Image will usually dominate content. Like it or not, it's a simple fact.

When people listen to a speaker or attend a seminar, they leave remembering only a few key points unless they have taken notes or recorded the event. They leave with impressions—images of the speaker—and judgments, such as, was the speaker prepared? Did he know what he was talking about? Did I like him?

Analyze your image very objectively and improve what you can improve. Today even your basic looks can be altered. Weight can be lost. Voice quality can be taught. Your style of dress tells a great deal about you—who you are and who you want to be. Image consultants can train you to improve your marketability by teaching you how to command attention by creating an image of a powerful presence.

You need to learn to create illusions. If you want to establish a successful New Age career, you're in show business, and you must create your act. Public speakers and seminar leaders who appear spontaneous have rehearsed to appear impromptu.

If you try to go out on stage and "just be yourself," you'll fail. As Arnold Zenker points out in his book *Mastering the Public Spotlight*, the real you couldn't tell the same stories over and over. You'd bumble around and couldn't appear spontaneous. You need to polish your act to perfection. That way, the show goes on even if you're sick, hungover, or jet-lagged, or if you've just had a fight with your spouse. Professional appearances are all illusion, rehearsed and contrived to work with precision. This awareness is related to any kind of career, product launch, or service offering.

Eric Hoffer's book *The True Believer* is often used to study charismatic leaders, mass movements, and the mindset of the joiners who are attracted to them. Hoffer lists the following qualities of personality necessary to be a leader of a mass movement:

Audacity and a joy in defiance.

An iron will.

A fanatical conviction that he or she owns the one and only truth.

A cunning estimate of human nature.

Faith in his or her own destiny.

A capacity for passionate hatred.

A belief that the present must be changed.

Delight in symbols, spectacles, and ceremonies.

Unbound brazenness, often expressed as a disregard for consistency. (Charlatanism of some degree is indispensable to effective leadership.)

An inner craving for a top leadership position.

The capacity to win and hold the loyalty of a group of able lieutenants.

He or she must be practical and a realist, yet must talk the language of a visionary and idealist.

He or she must have a devil. Hitler had the Jews. Fundamentalist Christian preachers have New Agers.

Ten Considerations to Increase Your Chances of Success

1. Appeal to others' self-interest. Find an angle for your customer to justify her expenditure. If what you offer will improve her life, help her be more attractive or more successful, or feel better about herself, she'll be a lot more likely to give you her credit card.

2. An old maxim says, "You can make a good living fulfilling people's needs, but if you want to get rich, offer them what they want."

3. Surround yourself with competent, responsible and supportive people. No one makes it to the top alone. No matter how smart, creative, or innovative you are, you need the assistance of others you can trust.

4. Give people more than they expect. When you always give something extra, something unexpected, you'll create lasting customers.

5. Think in terms of quality, not quantity. Quality always pays off in the long run.

6. Focus on detail. Success is the son of detail.

7. The longer the lead time you invest in your success, the greater your potential for payoff. All the extra energy and effort you put into what you're doing will pay off in time. Most people are oriented toward an immediate payoff. They cannot or will not wait.

8. Always think in terms of win/win. In dealing with others, unless both parties win, no one really wins.

9. Be persistent. Never give up. It's a lot more fun working toward the dream than it will be accomplishing it.

10. Work smarter, not harder. Statistics say you get 80 percent of your results in life from 20 percent of your efforts. So increase your efforts in the area that is paying off. Delegate to others the busy work that isn't generating the high percentage return.

Millionaire Time Tactics

Don't allow interruptions. Make this a priority. Get very tough about your time, or it can be eaten away by things other people think are important.

Set priorities, and do the most important things first. Group related activities together.

Divide big jobs into workable steps that you can take one at a time.

Concentrate on doing one thing at a time. Focusing all your energy in one direction is a powerful success force.

Eliminate busywork. This is work that doesn't really contribute to your overall success, although you take refuge in doing it because it's easy. Millionaires don't have time for busywork. When you do things that aren't worth doing, you delude yourself into thinking you've accomplished something.

Touch each paper only once. If you're going to read the memo or open the letter and read it, handle it immediately. Don't allow your desk to become a rotation center for paperwork.

Find ways to increase your speed and productivity. Use the latest technology, hire specialists, do whatever you need to do to do it faster and better.

Establish clear goals or a strong general direction. *Clear goals* means exactly that. Don't list something like, "Write a book someday," because "someday" lacks clarity. Chart your directions with a list, wall chart, or series of 3 x 5 cards that establish priorities. Stick to these priorities.

Drop unproductive things. If you start to watch a movie, do a research project, or start a book and it isn't good or isn't of value, don't feel you have to finish it. Don't continue to do anything that doesn't serve you. As you advance, you'll outgrow people, projects, and interests. When you do, let them go, so they don't hold you back.

If you have a staff, insist that when they bring you problems, they also bring you solutions to those problems.

Learn to say no. "No, I can't help you on that at this time." You only have so much time, and if you say yes to one thing, you're going to have to say no to something else. You decide what is important and how you're best served when it comes to your time.

Always respond to the most important people and projects first, not to which request came in first.

Finish all worthy projects fully.

Seven Important Steps to Take Immediately

1. **Project confidence.** Speak with authority and act confident, even if you don't feel that way. Some of the best new psychotherapies stress that you don't have to change how you feel about something to affect it as long as you're willing to change what you're doing. If you act confident even without feeling that way, soon your feelings will follow your new behavior, and you'll actually become confident.

2. Spend each moment doing the most productive thing you can. Stick little reminders on your bathroom mirror, the dashboard of your car, and on your desk: "I spend each moment doing the most productive thing I can to become a multimillionaire."

3. Establish role models in keeping with your desires. Role models prove that what you want to do can be done, which makes it easier for you to do it too. Learn everything you can about your role models. What motivates them? How do they work? Decide if their techniques are applicable to your personality.

4. Channel your thinking. Your ability to control and focus your thoughts is a major success factor. Losers focus upon lack and limitation rather than on abundance and success. If you're not creating your life with positive thoughts about yourself and your future, your subconscious mind is creating your reality based on past programming. That may not be desirable.

5. Develop laserlike concentration. Learn to focus your concentration at will while remaining alert and filtering out all thoughts unrelated to the current task. Millionaires all seem to have this ability. To develop it, use practice and exercises. Hypnosis audios are available. Meditation and martial arts exercises can help.

6. **Learn to say no firmly without offending.** Don't spread yourself too thin. By learning to say no in the beginning, you'll save yourself a lot of hassles down the line.

7. **Birds of a feather flock together.** If you want to be successful, surround yourself with successful people. Avoid negative people, socializers, and time wasters. If you want to accumulate wealth, associate only with those who are comfortable with abundance. Climbing the ladder of success usually means leaving some people behind—people who don't want you to succeed or who are envious of your accomplishments. Your success will make them appear to be failures.

Special Notes

To remain on track, use mind programming every day and sleep programming every night. You have to use the audio programs if you expect results. If you find that you're not willing to do this part of the work, you may have to face the fact that you're really not that interested in becoming a multimillionaire.

During the day, remind yourself over and over to do the most productive thing you can do to become a multimillionaire. Decide what the most productive thing is, and do it.

Daydream your dreams with intense emotion. When you tap into the emotion, you'll find your energy. Without inspired energy, it will be difficult to accomplish your goal.

Know the price of accomplishing your goal. It will be time, effort, money, or sacrifice—probably a combination of all four. Another way to look at this is through the law of balance: you must give something up to gain something.

Keep trying. The law of averages says that if you do twenty deals, you'll be twice as likely to hit a winner than if you set only ten deals in motion.

Learn how to become successful. To most people, this means developing a particular skill or launching a hot idea. But that's only part of success. Some experts claim that 90 percent of success results from four factors: energy, enthusiasm, self-image, and self-discipline.

You must have mental and physical energy to do what you need to do to succeed. Mental energy is necessary to learn your skills, calculate, and remember. Physical energy is the basis of all energy and is the key ingredient of renewal. How do you attain the energy you require? Basically, energy results from a lifestyle incorporating physical exercise and proper diet, plus a balance of work and play. A minimum of stress helps to assure an excess of physical energy.

Enthusiasm combined with action hastens success. Enthusiasm is the psychological adrenaline that drives you to success against the odds. It usually results from doing what you love to do. Before embarking on the quest for a goal, be sure you have the enthusiasm to see it through. The more you believe in your goal, the more enthusiasm you'll have.

You can do it. Now go do it!

Part 5

COLUMNS, 1979-2004

This section contains some miscellaneous columns that Dick wrote for his newsletter over several decades.

1979

The Power of the Mind: Metaphysical Questions

The following is an interesting dialogue, as it shows the thought process my husband went though after envisioning his Spirit Guide, Neeta, whom he says was a Native American woman. You can tell he was questioning many of the new, psychic experiences he and his clients and audience were going through, using his own wisdom and logic to answer questions. The following dialogue is Dick asking his Higher Self questions while in an altered state of consciousness.

If there is anything that my years of metaphysical investigation and psychic research has taught me, it is to never be amazed at the unlimited capabilities of the mind. It is generally agreed that we use no more than a few percentage points of our mental capabilities—maybe 5 percent. What about the remaining 95 percent? I am convinced that it is possible to contact a more knowledgeable portion of our totality which dwells in this Higher Mind. Call it super-conscious, the higher Self, God self, or another aspect, but there is an essence within us that is more aware than our waking consciousness.

To contact the Higher Self, you go into deep hypnosis and then use an additional technique to open a channel of direct communication with your own Higher Mind. Next, you send out a question and quietly listen as answers and often visions come back to you. Occasionally I go into an altered state with a tape recorder running so I can verbalize the responses. I do not know exactly where the information is coming from, but it is often phrased differently than I would express. Sometimes I have received new information which was later verified.

The following question and answer communications have to do with the power of the mind.

Question: Many books and organizations relate the experiences of individuals who had contact with the other side. Some general consistencies are common, but there are far too many inconsistencies for an objective investigator to accept. One says there are five levels, another seven, and each group designates different names for these levels. There are rays and guides and Sanskrit terms; every organization has its own esoteric dictionary. If you compare the words of psychic channels and researchers, you find the same problems. Edgar Cayce, Carlos Castaneda, Jane Roberts (Seth), Mark Probert, and numerous lesser-known teachers do not agree. What is nonphysical reality (after death) all about? Who do you believe?

Answer: All is mind. Each person experiences or glimpses their totality in a way that relates to them. If they keep it to themselves, then they have a psychic experience, but if the experience is published in a book or used as a foundation of an organization, there will always be joiners eager to accept it as truth. It was a symbolic truth to the person who experienced it, but that certainly doesn't mean that it relates to anyone else.

Question: Symbolic truth?

Answer: There is no such thing as Truth with a capital T. One religion is not right while all the rest are wrong. One belief is not closer to the truth than any other. Truth exists only as it relates to you. You ask who to listen to and who to believe. The only answer is yourself. If you see the other side as five levels which you must work your way through, then that is what you will find at death. If you see it as a burning hell, your mind can also arrange that. How about a mountain environment with creeks stocked with trout?

All is mind. As I have often said, "You do not have a mind; you are mind." The answer is that there is no answer at all except creativity. Entities exploring in the physical world are overpowered by that degree of freedom; thus they create elaborate belief systems to make themselves feel secure, and they cling to others who share their concepts as an additional crutch.

Let me ask you a question. Which of these three visions would you be most likely to relate to: an angel, a Native American woman, or an extraterrestrial spaceman?

Dick: A Native American woman, because I feel that relates to my reincarnation lineage.

Answer: All right. Let's say that another portion of you— call it your Higher Self—decides to communicate with the conscious you. The Native American woman vision would be a good medium to get your attention, would it not? But the man down the block might not accept a Native American woman or an angel as anything but a hallucination, but to him, a UFO or an extraterrestrial entity would be something worthy of sitting up and noticing.

Question: But would it not be there?

Answer: Not necessarily.

Question: How do you explain a situation in which several people see the same thing, such as a religious apparition? Let's take the case of the four young girls in San Sebastián de Garabandal in northern Spain in 1961. All four girls simultaneously went into ecstasies when an angel appeared. Tests showed they were all in trance and exhibited no reaction to physical pain. Each girl reported the same communications from the angel and the Blessed Virgin, who also appeared, and it created a minor worldwide sensation in the religion world.

Although thousands journeyed to the village to observe these regular occurrences, the apparitions were seen only by the girls and a thirty-six-year-old priest, who died a few hours after the experience. Those who observed the girls in ecstasy had no doubts as to the reality of their experience. Eventually, it was only one girl who continued to communicate with the Virgin. In 1963, she was told that a worldwide chastisement was forthcoming, but it would be preceded by a warning that would be visible all over the world, and there would be a great miracle which would take place at Garabandal. The sick who were present at the miracle would be cured and the sinners converted. The Virgin then explained that she had to go away, and there would be no more contact.

Answer: The answer can be summed up in one word: mind! Some apparitions are valid projections from one individual to another. Some people can project an effect. Their mind has the power to function as a reality projector, although they don't consciously realize it. They will be as amazed as everyone else at what they are observing, but they created the apparition and projected it to those attuned to their vibrational field, such as close friends or others on their frequency. In this case, maybe it was the priest. The common frequency could have been created by the common belief system.

Apparitions are usually the result of a very deep belief system. Combine your knowledge of the Catholic Church and sensitive young girls; then assume one girl has an exceptionally strong mind with extrasensory projection capabilities. You already understand the subtle possibilities of group hypnosis in a case like this.

Regarding the predictions which have not come to pass, you must realize that this is a standard pattern in such occurrences. The principals become consciously carried away with the transpiring events, but when something inside them realizes that they don't have the power to expand the ascent, the apparition says, "Goodbye," and the whole thing dissipates without the prediction coming to pass.

Question: So, if I saw the Native American woman, she would only be a creation of my own mind or someone else's?

Answer: I will answer yes, and then qualify it by saying that all is perspective. You might be dreaming in an altered state of consciousness or manifesting the reality through mental projection, or the energy essence (mind) of the Native American woman is projecting it to you. A nonphysical entity is just that—nonphysical; thus they are mind. So it is you who must perceive the physical form, nationality, and clothing. If you notice, there are very few people discussing naked apparitions, for they even project their own proprieties into their visions.

Question: But could a Native American woman who once lived on the earth and has since died . . . could she contact me?

Answer: Yes, under the proper conditions.

Question: Then how would you judge the experience?

Answer: If you must judge, I would think it would be by what was gained in the experience. Of course, if you have to have proof, as in the case of the girls in Spain, you could judge by the validity of the promised effect—the miracle.

Question: How do you explain situations in which people see the future when it does not directly relate to them? Such as a psychic seeing President Kennedy being shot, or an avalanche burying children in Europe?

Answer: There is no single answer. It would be generally accurate to say that sensitives were reading potentials, but there are other explanations. Remember that even among the nationally famous psychics, their predictions of this type are highly inaccurate. People forget about all the misses. If you have any doubts, dig out the January 1 issues of some of those supermarket tabloid newspapers. [I did, and the only accurate hits had to do with increased inflation and a few celebrity divorces.] These psychics are much more accurate when they work with individuals, for then they can read potentials directly from the minds of their clients.

Extrasensory perception certainly exists, and someone who has developed their ability in this area can read potentials more accurately. President Kennedy was hated and feared by many during a time of turmoil. Thus his potential for assassination was higher. There were hundreds of different assassination predictions for many different times. Yet the woman who is credited with trying to warn him not to go to Dallas missed on prophesying the outcome of a following presidential election.

As another example, a psychic in California told your friend Joanne that she would be riding her horse and the horse would hurt his foot. As it happened, her daughter Lynne was riding the horse when his foot was badly cut by a piece of barbed wire. Thus the prediction was partially accurate. Joanne had previously perceived the wire on one level of her mind but never gave it any thought consciously. Now that the horse was so important to her, it remained in the mind as a "charged" thought of potential danger. Since she went riding in the same general area every day, the potential for the accident was always there. The psychic perceived the potential and verbalized it. Psychics are more apt to perceive input that is emotionally charged, for it stands out in the mind. Thus relationship situations, joy, pain, and important experience predictions are most common.

Remember, Richard, many years ago when the Arizona psychic told you that your close friend in Minnesota had just had some difficult health problems, and you later found this to be true? I'm sure you now understand that since you and your friend were close, you were in superconscious communication and thus perceived important data from each other on a level above consciousness. The psychic simply told the information from your Higher Mind via extrasensory perception.

You see, each situation is different, but they can always be explained by the power of the mind, and everyone can develop these abilities if they are willing to take the time to do so. Out-of-body perceptions are often the explanation for a psychic experience. A man sleeping in the United States wakes up in a cold sweat because he dreams of an avalanche killing an entire lodge full of children. In the morning on the radio, he hears that the event actually transpired. The probable explanation is that while his mind was out traveling (astral projection) as his body slept, he was drawn to the situation by the terrible anguish that created a "charge" perceivable to anyone on the astral plane. He didn't dream what happened, he observed it.

There are also other explanations, such as "time warps" or "jumps," but they are unusual.

Question: All right. Let's move on to another area: the power of the mind to heal the body.

Answer: To say that the mind has the power to heal the body is incorrect. The mind has the power to help the body heal itself, but there is obviously a point beyond which it can[not] alter a deteriorating effect. Mental power in healing is a matter of relativity. Drugs never heal the body, for only the body can heal itself. Drugs or mental programming set the stage for the body to begin self-healing.

Question: What about the time David [Paladin, a good friend] was scheduled for open heart surgery, but he used psychic healing techniques, which worked and thus avoided the surgery? Or Greg's [another friend's] ability to eliminate the cancer in his body with self-hypnosis healing techniques?

Answer: There are good examples of aware individuals using the power of their mind while there was still time to do so. Had either condition progressed a little farther, it might not have been possible. Ideally, both men, after eliminating the problems, eliminated the conditions which weakened the body to allow these physical problems to develop. A positive mental attitude, no excessive stress, a proper diet, and exercise will enable a body to ward off most illness. This lifestyle will certainly accelerate self-healing if any problems do develop.

While the mind is using the physical body during an incarnation, it is a coexploration in which each is affecting the other. Your mind expands and grows as the result of a healthy body, and your body's peak performance comes through mind power.

Question: Do you mind if I quote that line?

Answer: How could the Higher Self mind if the lower self quoted him?

Question: Lower self? I'm not sure I like that term. Who am I really communicating with in these sessions?

Answer: Who do you want me to be?

Question: We could go on like this for a long time, couldn't we? Instead, let's communicate about the concept of mental reprogramming.

Answer: You're already a specialist at that subject. What exactly are you asking?

Question: I explain it to people from a technical perspective. How would you explain what transpires when someone uses hypnosis techniques to create a major change in their life?

Answer: The physical world is a reflection of your mind. As an example, take a man who grew up in abject poverty in a big city. From his youth, he felt that he didn't belong in such circumstances and envisioned owning a little house and a secondhand automobile. To achieve such a condition was a dream that would place him far above his peers. Today this is his reality: he owns a $15,000 house and a several-year-old car. Had he spent years dreaming of a $100,000 house and two new cars, he probably would have achieved that goal.

People feel they belong in certain circumstances, and the mind reflects their belief system in reality. Even if an individual loses everything, he will quickly find a way to reconstruct the envisioned environment.

Although most people would tell you they want more than they have or desire to alter certain circumstances, they didn't really feel they deserved it, or they subconsciously fear these results. Thus nothing changes. Reprogramming is a way to concentrate new pictures in the mind so that it begins to reflect a different reality.

Question: Thank you for sharing.
Answer: Anytime.

1980

You Can't Change What You Don't Recognize

Natural man analyzes: taking things and concepts apart to see how they tick. The Master of Life synthesizes: finding unity in diversity, wholeness in separateness, and seeing the oneness at the heart of things.

The problems of the world and our personal lives are so complex and overpowering that to resolve them, we must approach them in very simple and direct ways. New leaders, summit conferences, personal resolutions, and positive determination are not the answer. The solution lies in the creator of the conflicts, the creator of all the hate and fear: you and me.

We must come to. Understand that it is not the times, complications of society, or other people that cause us problems: it is our inability to cope with those things. It is resisting our life that causes our suffering.

Although most of us are discontent and desire change, this discontent, instead of creating an enthusiasm for change, causes most of us to lose our drive and become mediocre. That's why it's so important for us to discover our true Self.

Knowledge of the true Self cannot be given by another. We must inquire deeply within our own inner being.

Let's assume that you are ready for a radical transformation. You want your life to really start working. You desire to become all that you are capable of being. The first step is to understand yourself. Self-knowledge is the beginning of wisdom—the beginning of transformation.

To quote Zen teaching, "The true Self is found when the false Self is renounced." Without knowing the true Self, there can be no transformation. We must know our present Self not as we wish it to be, but as it is. If you are possessive and envious while deceiving yourself into believing you are not, facing the truth requires honesty and a clear mind. It is the first step towards transformation. You must know what you are, whatever it is: a bastard or a nice guy. Know it without distortion. Wisdom can only result through understanding *what is*. You can't change what you don't recognize.

What is is what you are. Not what you would like to be. Not your ideals. You need to express and explore your feelings and open up areas long forgotten and possibly painful, with the faith that the pain will release your vast potential for being all that you are capable of being—a potential for creativity and joy.

The problem with the majority of us is that we don't directly know ourselves. We avoid looking closely and seek the answers in systems, individuals, or ideologies. Yet the only answer is that the answer is you. You are the path; you are the way.

1980

Past-Life Regression—without Buck Owens

"When we are clear on our intent and get out of the way of the universe miracles can happen." I know that, and I've made the statement to numerous groups all over the country. I also tend to forget it. A one-day training in Salem, Oregon, last August served to remind me once again.

We rarely appear at functions other than those established and conducted by our own organization. Yet the enthusiasm of two Oregon sponsors was difficult to resist and the timing of a family vacation in Sunriver coincided perfectly. We contracted to do the one-day training and the sponsors supplied the location—a local high school. I was told the sound system was extremely good, and all we had to do was be there Sunday morning to coach the support team. Thus Trenna (my wife at the time) and I drove in from Portland, arriving in the small community about mid-morning. The seminar was to begin at 1:00 p.m. We planned to break for dinner and then wind it up by 8:00 p.m.

Upon our arrival, we met the seminar's sponsors, who explained that 417 people would be attending, plus miscellaneous guests and a support team of twenty. The seminar was supposed to be what Trenna and I call a "lay-down." No sweat, no effort, just go out there and do your thing.

We always carry our own microphones, so after coffee and casual conversation, I asked to hook into the sound system to do a mike check and trial run of the audio effects. After some initial confusion, a member of the school track team managed to crank up an ancient tube-type amplifier. I connected our equipment and was pleased to hear a commanding speaker system fill the auditorium with my voice. The only problem was that someone was also piping country music into the auditorium. "Can you turn off that music?" I asked.

"It doesn't turn off," replied the track star.

"Huh?"

"It's always on like that. Something about the old amplifier, I guess. We had a scientist speak here last week, and all through his talk we heard it just as loud as that. Dumb, huh? I really wish it was some good rock, then it wouldn't be so bad!"

I think it was the sound of Buck Owens wailing, "I've got a tiger by the tail" that did it. I yelled, "Hey, everybody, this isn't going to work. I can't conduct past-life regression and human potential processes on top of this."

"Are you sure?" asked one of the sponsors.

"I'm sure," I responded. "We seem to have a problem. What are we going to do about it in one hour? It's now noon and we need a new sound system."

The sponsor's eyes dilated. He took a deep breath and went into "survival." Survival is a state of nonfunctioning, usually induced by basic overwhelm. "Well, as you know,

Dick, Salem is just a little town, and even if everything were open, we don't have any place to rent sound equipment. We'll just have to make do."

"I understand that you think we'll have to make do, and it won't do." I walked around in a circle a few times in the center of the abandoned stage. When I stopped and looked around everyone had disappeared, except the track star, who was sitting slouched over a chair in his red running shorts and worn Nikes.

"I'm not doing any good here. I'll be out running around the track if you need me," he said, shuffling out the door.

Waylon Jennings had just finished a song, and the enthusiastic announcer was now expounding on the benefits of Red Wing chewing tobacco. Trenna was elsewhere, coaching the support team. I had the auditorium to myself. After some deep breathing, I sat down on the edge of the stage and whispered quietly, "I'm calling out to the positive powers of the universe and the unseen forces who share our energy. Hey, you guys, I give up. I'm getting out of the way, and if there is anything you can do to get this gig together, it will really be appreciated."

I looked up and watched a man sauntering down the aisle toward me. We exchanged greetings and small talk. He was a local plumber. His wife was interested in this kind of thing, and he was open to see what it was all about. While we were talking, the now sweaty track star wandered back in.

"You've got a music department in this school, don't you?" I asked.

"Yeah."

"Get a key. I want to see it."

"Why?"

"Because there is a possibility they may have some sound equipment."

"Well, even if they do, there is no way the school will let you use it."

"You're probably right, and I want you to get the key. Now."

Five minutes later I was wandering around in the music room, opening cabinets, examining closets, and there it was. Unbelievable! Beautiful! A Peavey amplifier, big enough to drive the large school speaker system. About this time the school janitor joined us.

"I'm going to use this amp for the seminar," I explained, picking it up.

"Not so fast, Sonny. Nobody touches anything in here unless the principal OKs it." He slammed his fist down to accentuate his statement.

"Where's the principal?"

"I dunno, probably in church. It's time for people to be in church, you know."

Five minutes later I found the seminar sponsor. "Please find the school principal and get permission for us to use the music department's amplifier. If you want a seminar here today, that is what is going to have to happen."

By this time, the participants were registering in the front hall. I waited in the open doorway of the office while the sponsor argued with the secretary of the local Baptist church. "Please have him come to the phone. It surely won't interrupt the service if you go in quietly and ask him to come to the phone. Yes . . . a reincarnation seminar. No,

Ma'am. I assure you it isn't the devil's work. No. Yes. I know people should be in church. Please . . ."

I usually change into a suit just before going on stage, but at this time I was still wearing worn Levis and a T-shirt. Two women were now loitering in the hall a few feet away. I overheard one explain to the other, "He's the one who's going to do it to us . . . but he's pretty sloppy looking, isn't he? You'd think for something like this he could at least find some jeans that didn't have holes in them."

Trenna wandered in, "Richard, why aren't you dressed? We go on in less than a half hour?"

"We have permission to use the equipment," the sponsor, emerging, exclaimed happily. Five minutes later, it was in place on stage. Components matched. No more country music, and our tape equipment functioned perfectly. I went to plug in the microphones.

"I don't believe it. Our mikes all have cannon plugs and the amp is rigged for standard phone plugs. I didn't bring any conversion transformers."

Trenna replied calmly, "I know you don't like to use other microphones, but why not use theirs this time around? You've got to admit that a little less quality in the audio is better than a past-life with Buck Owens."

The janitor and track star stood watching. "Where are your microphones?" I asked.

"Don't have any." They both shrugged. Then the track star's eyes lit up. He left and returned with a very small microphone. It was the kind that comes with a cheap cassette tape recorder and had a two and a half foot cord.

Trenna broke up. "Richard, if you want to conduct the seminar hunched over beside the amplifier, it will work fine." she laughed.

"Twenty minutes to go," someone yelled. "They're letting them into the auditorium now."

"Trenna, there is no way we can do this gig without a microphone or with country music. Now we need a cannon plug conversion transformer," I said in my saddest tone of voice.

"We got a music store downtown," I heard a voice say. It was the plumber I'd talked with before. "It's only about three minutes away."

"Won't it be closed on Sunday?" I asked.

"Probably."

"OK, let's go for it." I ran after him in the car. A cannon plug conversion transformer is a very specialized piece of professional equipment. I only know of a couple of places in all of Phoenix where I might find one. In following the plumber, I was convinced that I'd gone into survival, but there didn't seem to be a lot of alternatives. As we drove into the downtown section, it was obvious that everything was closed.

"There it is, up there," said my newfound friend, pointing to a sign for a piano and organ company above a storefront. The store was dark. Yet as we drove up in front of it, a man emerged, quickly relocked the door, and ran to his waiting car at the curb. We screeched to a stop, and I ran over to him.

"Please wait. We're looking for a special piece of equipment and . . ." I explained the entire story.

He told me that all he did was repair musical instruments for the store. While working at home, he had run out of some needed parts. He didn't know anything about sound equipment, but he did agree to go back into the store and call the owner. As we accompanied him inside, I looked around and felt my stomach drop. It wasn't the kind of store likely to carry professional equipment of this type.

The owner was now on the phone, and by coaching the repair man, I communicated our needs. The owner explained that he thought maybe they did have one of those things. It would be way down in the back of a bottom drawer, in the cabinet along the west wall. I followed and watched over the repairman's shoulder as he began to go through the bottom drawers. "Oh, my Gawd. There it is. I don't believe it. Impossible . . ."

My heart sank again when I looked at the price tag. I didn't have that much cash on me. Neither did the plumber. "Can I leave you my credit card, my watch and rings, anything? "

The repair man explained the situation to his boss, who replied, "Oh, that's all right. Just let them take it on approval, and they can bring it back on Monday. No big deal."

I slipped into my suit as the clock hit 1:00 p.m. and then spent a minute or so silently thanking the unseen for supporting us once again.

Bonding in Hypnosis

Two people who simultaneously hypnotize each other can together achieve a somnambulistic level that leads to intense bonding and mental telepathy. This was the tentative conclusion of a study conducted by Dr. Charles Tart and reported in the book *Supersenses* by Charles Panati.

The study was conducted at the University of California at Davis with two psychology graduate students, Anne and Bill. Before beginning the experiment, Anne and Bill were casual acquaintances. Each of them was proficient in hypnotic induction and techniques.

The experiment involved three hypnosis sessions in which Anne and Bill were to take turns hypnotizing each other to ever deeper levels. Both had been preconditioned by Tart that he would orchestrate their experience and would be able to communicate with either of them simply by placing his hand on their shoulders.

During the first experiment, Tart was gratified to find out it was possible for Anne and Bill to hypnotize each other. The system they used to determine trance depth was for each individual to subconsciously rate the depth on a scale of 1 to 50, with 50 being the deepest-level trance. In the first experiment, after several minutes of hypnotic volleying, Anne reported a trance depth of 40, while Bill reported a depth of 36.

Tart wanted them to go even deeper. He placed his hand on Anne's shoulder and instructed her to have Bill deepen her trance. After about ten minutes, Anne reported a depth of 43. Tart then asked Bill to restate his trance depth. Bill responded with 43. *On his own, he had gone to the same depth as Anne.*

Tart decided to take it even further, so, placing his hand on Anne's shoulder, he instructed her to take Bill down even further. She did not respond. Finally, after several alarming minutes, Tart was able to make contact with her. He asked why she hadn't responded to his suggestion. "I did," she answered, explaining that she was walking down a flight of stairs and deepening his trance with each step. Of course Tart asked her to do it aloud so Bill could hear her and walk with her. Anne indignantly replied that Bill was with her; he could hear her. Tart wanted to find out if this was true, so he placed his hand on Bill's shoulder and asked for a depth report. In a faraway voice Bill answered: "57." *As a result of Anne's seemingly silent induction, Bill had gone into significantly deeper trance.* In addition, his body was inert and his breathing faint: two sure signs of a somnambulistic trance.

Tart realized that he had already gotten more than he bargained for, so he instructed Anne and Bill to dehypnotize each other by counting backwards from their trance level.

The second hypnosis session soon followed. After several minutes of mutual induction, Bill decided to deepen Anne's trance by creating a fantasy journey. In the fantasy, he and Anne were standing on the side of a mountain in front of the entrance to a tunnel. As they walked hand-in-hand into the tunnel, Bill suggested that with each step, they would both go into deeper trance.

What Bill didn't say was that with each step they would also move further and further into their own private world. Tart became an outsider whose intrusions were resented. Sometimes Bill would not respond to Tart's questions at all; at other times his replies were curt and hostile.

Tart decided on an innovative approach to sharing their world. He asked both Anne and Bill to find something in the tunnel to bring back to him. Bill, who had been so difficult to communicate with, was instant in his vehemence that nothing was to leave the tunnel. Tart repeated his order to Anne, who wanted to comply. Bill sternly forbade her, and in fact began counting her out of her trance. Tart had never given Bill an order to do this!

In the postsession interviews, it became clear that the tunnel was entirely Bill's property. Bill stated he felt the tunnel had rules of its own, which restricted taking anything out of it.

An even more interesting result of the second session was its effect on Anne and Bill. The strong rapport they had established during mutual hypnotic consciousness seemed to last well beyond the session. According to Tart, "Anne and Bill developed an intense friendship . . . they felt extremely close to one another as a result of their shared experience." From casual classmates, Anne and Bill had become inseparable friends, spending a great deal of time together.

Although Anne and Bill clearly enjoyed their new relationship, others did not—especially Anne's husband and Bill's wife. Friction in both their marriages, however, did not prevent the third session from occurring.

In this session, Anne and Bill wasted no time entering a fantasy world of their own. They labeled the place Heaven, and each of them described the water as "like champagne, and had beautiful, huge bubbles in it." It was clear from their descriptions they were both seeing the same things. Once again, Bill felt the place had its own rules. He did not want Anne to divulge how they got there. Suddenly, Bill decided it was time to leave. When Anne argued to remain, he began counting her back up.

Afterwards, both Anne and Bill talked of feeling disembodied, of being able to float through each other. Tart described their experience as "a partial blending of themselves quite beyond the degree of contact human beings expect to share with others."

This partial blending of Anne and Bill began to spill over into their personal lives more and more. They were able to telepathically anticipate each other's wishes when they were together; even when they were apart, Bill would suddenly know what Anne was doing, or vice versa. They were almost always correct. In fact, the degree of rapport between Anne and Bill, and of strife between them and their respective spouses, grew to such an extent that they had to dissolve their friendship and abandon further hypnotic sessions.

The case of Anne and Bill is not an isolated incident. A few months later, Tart attempted the same experiment with another pair who were also married to other individuals. The same sequence of events occurred: strong friendship, a shared world, and telepathic bonds. This experiment also grew too intense to be continued.

From his experiments, Tart concluded that, between people sharing the same state of consciousness, "ESP is a function of the number of barriers let down."

1982

Aphorisms for Relationships

Love each other as you would be loved, cherishing the passion and joy while allowing the negativity to flow through you without affecting you.

Acceptance
Treasure each other's uniqueness and accept each other as you are without expectations of change.

Commitment
Totally commit to your relationship—mentally, physically, spiritually, emotionally, and financially. Withholding reflects doubts that will undermine the foundation of your union.

Support
Support each other in ways that increase self-esteem. This is critical to a good relationship, for to love another, you must love yourself.

Detachment

Let the little things go. Before reacting negatively, ask your-self, "Does it really matter, or am I just acting out of a need to be right?"

Communication

Openly communicate, and share yourself. The greatest gift you can give to each other is to be all of who you are. Be willing to discuss needs and compromise solutions.

Listen

Listen to each other and be willing to appreciate the oth-er's position, even when you don't agree. Also, learn to hear what isn't being verbalized.

Comfort

Be of comfort to each other in the midst of worldly con-cerns. Be friends as well as lovers; make your union a refuge of balance and harmony.

Transcend Anger

Rise above anger by saying to yourself, "I am angry because I had expectations of gaining approval or control in this sit-uation. These are not my rights."

Time

Always make time for each other and find fulfillment in the current moment. Shared activities are the building blocks of a good relationship.

Transcend Blame

Blame is an expression of self-pity and is incompatible with the acceptance of karma. Everything is karmic, so the situation was self-created to test your level of awareness.

Spirituality

Encourage each other to evolve spiritually. In this way, you can transcend the darkness and attain peace of mind.

The Pain in Your Life

Most people experience a great deal of pain in their lives: pain from their physical and emotional burdens, pain in their relationships or lack of relationships, pain from failure, rejection, or unfulfilled needs.

Sadly, we're conditioned to learn through pain, not love. We learn to think and act in a self-actualized way by experiencing the pain. After a few lifetimes, we intuitively learn what makes life painful and what makes it work. We learn that wisdom erases karma and that we can set ourselves free now!

1983

When the Lesson Is Learned

Stated simply, we reincarnate for the opportunity to learn. And I must often remind myself of this fact. It is so easy to become complacent in a comfortable position and resist change. Yet change will always come—often when you least expect it.

We need to remember that if everything remained constant and never changed, it would eventually stagnate, just like a standing pool of water. From a karmic perspective, what happens specifically is not important—how we react to what happens is the basis of whether or not we have increased our level of awareness.

What you would call a negative situation in your life is only a problem if you look upon it as a problem. As I have taught for years in my Bushido SST Seminar, we can all transform the way we experience our life, or in other words, change our perspective. As difficult as it may be to accept, our problems actually contribute satisfaction to our lives. If there were no problems to challenge you, there could be no growth. There would be no way for you to learn how to handle things and become aware of your capability for making your life work.

In fact, if you didn't have problems, you'd have to invent some to give yourself the opportunity to grow and learn to make your life work. And obviously that is often what we do. We manifest problems, not consciously, but subconsciously we create these challenges.

The real secret to growth through problems is to look upon problems as opportunities. The bigger the problem, the bigger the opportunity. And the problem usually stays with us just as long as we need it to achieve an understanding of ourselves and others. Once we have that understanding, we can let go of the effect.

In many problem situations, nothing about the situation will change but our viewpoint. And yet, by changing our reaction to the situation, we eliminate the problem. Things may be at their worst, yet we remain happy. Each time we rise above a painful situation, we have attained soul growth, which I perceive as intuitive strength and awareness. Hopefully this awareness will make future problems of the same kind unnecessary. "When the lesson is learned, the experience is unnecessary" is one of my favorite metaphysical sayings.

1986

My First Success Seminar Was a Failure Until . . .

What does success mean to you?
- Monetary wealth
- Fame and respect
- Peace of mind
- A good relationship
- A career you enjoy

"Success seminars aren't very successful," I was told by a man who made his living conducting them. "People leave excited and highly motivated, but their enthusiasm soon fades without constructive change," he explained.

At the time, I was investigating motivational and success seminars in preparation for my own. I'd been conducting reincarnation gatherings and the Bushido Training for years, and felt I could combine hypnosis programming and Bushido techniques to create a very successful success seminar!

As an expression of that confidence, participants were offered a money-back guarantee. The seminar was expensive, and sixty-five people attended the first three days in

Los Angeles. The majority were already successful by most standards, but wanted to experience a greater degree of success or change life directions. Yet they were all hesitating to take the steps to generate change.

Each participant was given a goal sheet asking many questions including, "Exactly what do you want to achieve?" "List your primary goals in order of importance." They filled out the sheets, and my challenge was to assist them in manifesting the goals.

This was my mistake.

As the seminar progressed, I often used processing (questioning) techniques on individuals who asked questions about their goals. They claimed to know what they wanted, but under questioning, the goals crumbled. By the time I was one and a half days into the seminar, it was obvious that the majority of the participants didn't really know what they wanted. They thought they did. They told me they did. But there was no clarity of intent. If they didn't know exactly what they wanted, how could they expect to ever attain it? My participants were fighting themselves every step of the way.

I'll never forget the room-service lunch in my hotel room that noon—I sat staring at it, too upset to eat. If I followed my notes and proceeded according to my outline, the training wouldn't work. I went into self-hypnosis and asked for guidance.

That afternoon, I went back into the seminar ballroom without notes and conducted the rest of the seminar based only on my own trainer instincts and, very possibly, a lot of help from the other side.

The seminar was a success, according to the enthusiastic participants. One man asked for his money back (he was expecting a motivational seminar). In those years that followed, many of those who attended have written or attended other seminars and have related fabulous success stories relating from the awareness they received that weekend.

It was also obvious that motivators had the cart before the horse. They'd skipped the all-important preparatory phase of self-examination. It was like attempting to teach algebra without first teaching basic mathematics.

In those three days of my first Success Seminar, I found several basic subconscious blocks that were keeping people from attaining what they wanted. There were many minor blocks, and most of the attendees were violating one or more of the "basic tenets of success." Armed with this awareness, and investigative and programming techniques, I found it easy to conduct a powerful and successful seminar—and I went on to conduct it in all major cities in 1981 and 1982.

I no longer conduct the Success Seminar in person, because I prefer to focus my communication efforts on more spiritual, Zen-based training, and there are only so many weekends per year. Although it isn't possible to communicate the trainer-participant interaction that takes place in the seminar room, it is easy to impart the general awareness and to provide the materials for you to process yourself.

1989

You Are the Message

What is success? For one person it's wealth, for another it's career satisfaction.

Someone else wants recognition, and I know people who measure success by their personal freedom or their level of awareness. To others, success means a loving relationship. But true success means all of these things. I don't think you should settle for anything less!

Within the first seven seconds of initially meeting someone, each of you, both directly and indirectly, communicate a world of information as your read and test each other. You are the message! Research shows that we start to make up our minds about other people within these first seven seconds.

In my Success Seminars, New Age Career Seminars, and the annual Professional Hypnotist Training, I teach the participants about posturing, positioning, the importance of an image and brain/mind techniques. Much of this awareness is from my advertising years (1958 to 1975), working for major ad agencies and heading my own creative service organization.

Effective advertising is the power of persuasion. In 1974, I sought to expand my understanding of this power by studying brain/mind technology and hypnosis. The interest became a full-time career in 1976, when I began writing books about my experiences, creating hypnosis tapes and conducting seminars.

While in the process of creating my Power Your Mind Seminar (which was presented for six mornings at the 1989 Transcendence Training in Palm Springs), I'd been going through years of notes and studying the works of such master communicators as Arnold Zenker, Al Ries, Jack Trout, and David Ogilvy. The following are a few examples of the kind of awareness that can be applied to your career and personal life.

When you communicate with others, you project your message in several ways: with the words you use, with your eyes, your facial expressions and body language, and your voice, including the pitch, tone, volume, and intensity. Your commitment to your words is also measured, your sense of humor is a factor, and there are numerous additional signals that you send out to complete the message. You are a composite message—a walking, talking billboard, and the product you are selling is yourself. Your acceptance of this fact determines whether or not you're going to get what you want out of life.

Can the message be improved? Most likely, the answer is yes. So start by identifying your best qualities—those that communicate a positive message. You must always be *who you really are*, but be at your best.

The four essentials of a great communicator are:

1. Be prepared so that you can project absolute confidence.
2. Be comfortable with yourself; it'll make other people feel comfortable with you as well.
3. Be committed. When you care about what you say, you'll say it well and with passion.
4. Be interesting. It's difficult to be interesting if you're not committed and vice versa.

Charisma is the ability to subtly cause other people to react to you instead of you reacting to them. Charismatic people control the atmosphere by setting the speed of the communications. Pause and pace your rate of speech to maximize the impact. Don't fear silence. Use gestures; move effectively and assertively. Use your eyes expressively and display a full range of emotions.

Deliberately modulate your voice and look directly into the eyes of your audience. These ideas relate to one-on-one communications as well as talking to hundreds of people. When you control the atmosphere, you project a likable fearlessness, without arrogance. Once you've developed this ability, it will carry you far beyond charisma.

Image maker Arnold Zenker reminds us of the old adage, "Sell the sizzle, not the steak!" By this he means to sell the image, not the information. As Arnold Zenker says in *Mastering the Public Spotlight*, "On television, in live appearances, in interpersonal contacts, it's the image of you that counts."

Is this external you any less real than the internal personality you know and cherish? To the contrary. Dr.

Willard Gaylin, professor of clinical psychiatry at Columbia University, focuses on the issue:

> The inside of a man represents another view, not a truer
> one. A man may not always be what he appears to be,
> but what he appears to be is always a significant part
> of what he is . . . the inner man is fantasy. If it helps you to
> identify with one, by all means do so. Like any fantasy, it
> serves your purpose alone. It has no standing in the real
> world, which we share with each other. Those character
> traits, those attitudes, that behavior—that strange and
> alien stuff sticking out over you—that's the real you!

Zenker also stresses that image will usually dominate content. Like it or not, it's a simple fact. When people listen to you, they leave remembering very little of what was actually said. But they will remember their impressions, their images of you. They will remember if they liked you, if they thought you were knowledgeable, and if you made sense.

1989

Programming

Your personality is the sum total of all of your past programming and interaction of three factors: *traits*, *habits*, and *viewpoints*. These factors aren't genetically inherited, they are acquired: *thus they are alterable with new programming*. If you sincerely desire to change because you realize your message isn't working, you can do it with brain/mind reprogramming techniques.

There are eight primary brain/mind techniques to program your subconsciousness mind to get what you want. Once you know exactly what you want and commit yourself to using all the techniques regularly, the faster you will obtain results. The eight techniques are:

1. Hypnosis programming
2. Sleep programming
3. Subliminal programming
4. Goal imprinting (self-talk)
5. Dream programming
6. Visual support materials (goals printed and placed where you will see them regularly)

7. Role models (someone who is very successful at what you want to do)
8. Behavior changes

The new Zen-based psychotherapies, such as Morita Therapy and Reality Therapy, advise that you don't have to change how you feel about something in order to affect it, as long as you are willing to change what you are doing. If you change your behavior, your attitude will soon fall in line with the new behavior.

1989

Accelerate Learning and Skills

Unlike your conscious mind, your subconscious has no power of choice. By its very nature, it must do as instructed, which includes assisting you to make changes and accelerate skill.

In 1971 and 1972, I studied hypnosis with a masterful metaphysician and hypnotist named Don Weldon, of Creative Guidelines in Phoenix, Arizona. I took all his basic classes and went on to his advanced series. By loaning me a home-made hypnosis cassette tape to alleviate a head cold, Don inspired my experiments with astral projection tapes, which I then gave to life-term prisoners at the Florence, Arizona penitentiary.

Group explorations, along with self-explorations, followed as I attempted to learn the full potential of an altered state of consciousness. This included studying the works of several established hypnotists. The most visible at the time was Melvin Powers, the author of numerous books on hypnosis published by his own company, Wilshire Books. Melvin graciously agreed to see me in his North Hollywood office, and our conversation proved to be one of those life-influencing events that you never forget.

At that time, Wilshire Books was a very successful company, publishing hundreds of self-improvement books, including the international bestseller, *Psycho-Cybernetics* by Maxwell Maltz. The company also published books on metaphysics, chess, Jewish heritage, vegetarianism, and an entire library for horse lovers.

The most memorable part of our meeting was Melvin's personal success formula. Although I can't remember his direct quote, the essence of what he said was, "I only publish books about things I am passionately interested in. That way I have high energy for the projects, and the energy converts to success." This is a formula I have followed in my own publishing efforts.

Melvin also told me about many of his personal experiments with hypnosis and why he had become so fascinated with the subject. "The experiment that really did it," he said, "was to hypnotize myself, then open my eyes, scan a page of *Newsweek* for a few seconds, close my eyes and tell myself, 'You will remember every word on the page exactly as it was written.' Then I'd awaken and recite the page, word for word."

Before I left, Melvin gave me a tour of his publishing company and warehouse, and a phonograph record of his voice directing an induction and awakening to teach the technique. It was very well produced, using a metronome for pacing.

Although the possibility of a market for individual hypnosis tapes was taking form in my mind, I was far too busy with my creative service business and publishing books for the professional advertising market. Then, in 1976, the success of my book *You Were Born Again to Be Together* generated so much mail, I had to hire a secretary just to answer it. To pay for the secretary, I created a few hypnosis tapes in June 1976 and sold them via an advertising flyer included with the responses. No one had ever heard of hypnosis tapes, and the orders rolled in.

The new business soon took over the old, and I devoted all my time to exploring the potentials of hypnosis, conducting seminars and writing about the results and my experiences.

Many people came to me with special requests involving the acceleration of skill. At that time I lived in Scottsdale, Arizona, the winter home of a professional baseball team, and the players sought advice on visualization and programming techniques. A songwriter wanted a tape to generate more creativity. Others wanted to increase confidence, or persistence, or their reading rate. We got results, and experimented continually to find ways to get better results.

By late 1977, I was running crude subliminal video experiments that in some cases proved so successful that they scared me. The first big success showed visuals of a child getting younger and younger until it was an embryo in the womb. The images were flashed on the screen so quickly that only a blip was consciously perceived. I told the seminar participants nothing about what they were going to experience. They were simply instructed to watch the large screen video projection with their eyes open while I induced an altered state. Most of the viewers experienced spontaneous regressions to the time of their birth or back to being in the womb.

A forty-year-old woman observed her mother attempting to abort her. Upset by the regression, she left the seminar
room to call her mother, now seventy, to ask, "Did you try
to abort me before I was born?" She went on to describe the
exact method her mother used. The mother began to cry
and confessed that she had indeed attempted an abortion
exactly as her daughter had experienced in an altered state.

In 1978, my involvement with Kenpo karate became
the testing ground for experiments in accelerating skill
by watching moves perfectly performed on a large-screen
video while listening to a beta-to-theta follow response and
verbal suggestions.

Eighteen years later, in 1989, the one thing that continues to amaze me more than anything else is the incredible
power of the subconscious mind. It is the willing servant of
the person who intelligently directs it. Like the biocomputer
it is, the subconscious always generates a personal reality
that reflects these directions.

Freud said, "The unconscious (subconscious) knows
nothing of reason or logic." Brain/mind researchers have
proven how correct he was. Your subconscious mind doesn't
care if you get what you want out of life or not. If what you
want happens to match what you've been programmed to
get, fine. If it doesn't, fine. It's up to you to supply the correct programming. If you don't, you have no one to blame
but yourself.

What are the power limits of the subconscious mind?
No one knows. It all depends on how it is used by the conscious mind. We know it is self-starting and self-directing,
as generated by your thoughts, emotions, and program-

ming. If you aren't experiencing life as you would like it to be, your past thoughts and emotions have generated beliefs that are limiting your subconscious mind's ability to function. Thankfully, these undesirable beliefs can usually be altered with programming to make your subconscious support your conscious desires.

To successfully direct subconscious mind power requires a sustained and consistent effort. Programming takes the form of focused desire, positive thoughts, and altered state of consciousness sessions. All must be applied purposefully and systematically. The subconscious mind can't override the need to study, practice, and prepare, and it can't replace clear, consistent, rational thinking. But when you know exactly what you want with no indecisiveness at all, and if you're willing to make the effort to support your goal, you're well over halfway there, and your subconscious will carry you the rest of the way.

1989

More Universal Laws

My husband's articles about Universal laws were among the most popular in his magazine, Master of Life Awareness. *He had written about twenty primary laws, but because so many readers wrote to him asking about the others, he drafted what he considered to be the fifty primary laws and sold it as a one-hour audiotape. He also included this list as a hand-out to his professional hypnotism students.*

The Universe is perfectly balanced by natural and moral laws, which are regulatory vibrations to maintain order. When you work within the laws, you can be assured of an eventual positive outcome.

The laws almost become a complete metaphysical system to which you can refer about any problem. As such, it is an ideal basis for counseling yourself and others. There are hundreds of Universal Laws that can assist you in the self-creation process. The following laws are a few that will best serve you in creating your own reality.

The Law of Commitment

When you become clear on your intent, making a decision and obligating yourself to a goal, everything begins to fall into place. Once you have pledged this direction, things begin to happen almost magically, as if you were a magnet drawing into your experience that which is needed for manifestation. The secret of this success power is *to have an urgent, insistent desire for what you want and no indecisiveness at all.* The greater your emotional desire, the more rapidly you will experience the reality.

The Law of Reflection

This law states that the traits you respond to in others are those that you recognize in yourself, both positive and negative. The four primary manifestations are:

1. What you admire in others, you recognize as existing within yourself.
2. What you resist and react to strongly in others is sure to be found within yourself.
3. What you resist and react to in others is something that you are afraid exists within yourself.
4. What you resist in yourself, you will dislike in others.

In other words, other people are a mirror in which you can see yourself . . . if you have the self-awareness to look.

The Law of Dissonance

You will experience mental discomfort when you hold conflicting beliefs or when your actions don't agree with your beliefs. As an example, you believe that smoking is bad for your health, but you continue to smoke. You believe that extramarital affairs are morally wrong, but you continue to be involved with someone outside your marriage. You believe that you should be more patient with your children, but you continue to yell at them.

This law says that when your beliefs and actions are incompatible, you will attempt to reduce the resulting discomfort by changing either your actions or your beliefs. The smoker will either become an ex-smoker or will deny or rationalize the health threat. The adulterous spouse will either stop the behavior or rationalize it, maybe saying, "What my spouse doesn't know won't hurt him or her. Anyway, since my needs have been fulfilled, I'll be a better partner." The impatient parent either changes the impatient behavior or rationalizes the attitude by saying, "It's better for me to yell and release the anger than to repress it." The Law of Dissonance is sometimes called the Law of Self-Delusion.

The Law of Experience

New information entering your mind supersedes previous information of a similar nature. Once a pathway has been established in your brain, the information it contains will remain, unless new information overrides it.

As an example, while horseback riding, you fall off and hurt yourself. If that is the end of your equestrian experience, it has been programmed negatively. That's why instructors always urge new riders to climb back on the horse immediately after falling off. You need fresh, new input to erase the trauma of the fall. This law is an innate, organic process that does not require your conscious attention or active participation. The basic processes of the brain are in an endless state of growth and reorganization.

The Law of Experience can be used effectively in altered state of consciousness programming because your subconscious mind cannot tell the difference between a fantasy and a real experience. As an example, if you suffer from agoraphobia (fear of crowds), enter an altered state and vividly imagine yourself being perfectly relaxed while in a crowd. Your mind will accept this as reality and invoke the Law of Experience. A few weeks or months of this programming will overcome the old, fearful programming and your mind will believe that you are calm in crowds and act accordingly.

The Law of Fearful Confrontation

If you fear doing something and have the courage to do it anyway, your mind will soon perform a flip-flop, and you may even become addicted to doing it. Let's say you fear skydiving but force yourself to do it. The exciting experience generates the internal release of beta-endorphins, which are internally manufactured chemicals resembling opium and are quite addicting. The more you skydive, the more you will want to skydive. This applies to any exciting, internally stimulating experience, such as downhill skiing, business gambles, or whatever it was that you originally feared. Knowing how this law works allows you either to use it or resist it—whatever you decide is appropriate to the situation.

The Law of Dominant Desire

A stronger emotion will always dominate a weaker one. Every idea you perceive is the beginning of a manifestation, though not all ideas are expressed in reality. It doesn't matter what idea you consciously favor or even know to be desirable; the stronger emotion will begin to permeate all aspects of your life. The idea is to be consciously aware of where your dominant desires are leading you.

The Law of Environment Manifestation

Everything that surrounds you is an extension of you. Your mate, children, home, furniture, car, pets, yard, office, and career are all physical expressions of the belief system and attitudes you have. Your environment is a reality picture of your core beliefs, expressing your self-image and cultural overview. What can you learn about yourself by examining your environment?

The Law of Resistance

What you resist, you draw to yourself and perpetuate its influence in your life. Resistance is fear, so it is something you need to resolve. The Law of Resistance ensures that you will encounter the fear over and over again until you learn to let go of the fear through conscious detachment.

The Law of Self-Worth

Your self-esteem is critical to your happiness and success: you only attract what you feel you deserve. The truth is that you are not what you have and you are not what you do. Beneath your fear programming, you are already perfect. You are already a fully self-actualized individual. As you rise above the fear-based emotions through conscious detachment, you will experience increased self-esteem, resulting in more options. The more options you have, the more risks you can take, leading to still more opportunities to rise above fear-based emotions through conscious detachment, and so on. The better you like yourself, the better others will like you, and the more worth you will feel.

The Law of Growth

Growth is born out of the agitation of discontent, which will develop when you've reached a level where there is no new challenge. Carefully study your dissatisfactions; they will tell you what you are about to leave behind and may also point to future directions.

The Law of Self-Truth

Truth is what works for you. If you believe something to be so, it becomes law for you. Be very careful about what you accept to be the truth, for it will influence all aspects of your life.

The Law of Release

Let go—without regret or resentment—of anything that is no longer useful and purposeful. This includes such things as books, philosophy, clothing, beliefs, lifestyle, associations, and so on. Pleasure should be in the moment of the experience. By letting go of something when it is no longer useful, you free yourself to start another learning experience.

1990

Getting Negative about Negativity

Basic human rights, from a Master of Life perspective, allow for expression rather than repression. One of these is your right not to be subjected to negativity.

Have you ever noticed how many people make their living from negativity—trashing people, products, and ideas? Did you watch the *60 Minutes* television shows reporting on all the inferior American weapons manufactured by inferior American companies? How many times have you heard that the American military can't do anything right? Well, the critics have certainly been proven wrong on that one. Of course, it won't stop them. Never mind that it isn't accurate.

Personally, I've had enough of listening to negativity. I don't intend to read another business article about our inability to compete with the Japanese, or how we've lost our spirit, or that the trade deficit is ruining our economy, or that Nostradamus predicted that the Gulf War was just the beginning of terrible things to come. In regard to all these things, the good news is that the bad news is wrong.

I'm even through reading the movie critics. If I had listened to *The New York Times* and *Entertainment Weekly*, I wouldn't have gone to *Dances with Wolves*, and I would have missed one of the best movies I've ever seen. Almost every critic trashed the film *Flatliners*. I thought it was extremely good and made many valid metaphysical points. I won't go into the recent films the critics have loved and I despised.

So often over the years, when I've been interviewed by the media, the reporter will admit that his editor won't allow him to write a positive piece on the New Age unless it's tongue in cheek. So scratch the hope of any positive stories on esoteric subjects in the mainstream media.

Gossip, sarcasm, and exposé sell a lot of newspapers and inflate television ratings. *60 Minutes* is rarely out of the top ten. And look at the other tabloid TV news shows, much less the tabloids themselves. *The National Enquirer* remains one of the largest circulation publications in the country.

I don't want to belabor negativity. I want to remind you that a lot of influential people (including politicians) make their living by being negative. And when you listen to them, you may not be serving yourself.

Metaphysics 101 teaches that you create your own reality with your thoughts.

Your mind operates like a computer, and your thoughts are your software. Relating this concept to computer terminology, it's GIGO—garbage in, garbage out. Feed your mind negativity, and you'll experience negativity in your life. It's simply cause and effect—karma.

Most people have no idea how much time they spend thinking negatively about routine aspects of their life. Even less do they realize how often they allow the media to influence them into more negativity than they already experience.

You're probably thinking more negative thoughts than positive ones. If that's so, there is simply no way you can be creating anything but a negative reality. With all that negative computer programming, how could it do anything but create more negativity? This may take the form of depression, vague feelings of unease, relationship problems, career problems, sickness, or physical problems, and on and on.

Reality/Fantasy Tests

Your subconscious mind (the memory bank that accepts the programming) can't tell the difference between thoughts and things, reality and fantasy, real experiences and imagined experiences. The brain/mind researchers proved this a long time ago by recording brain wave patterns under specific conditions. Test subjects were placed in a room and connected to an EEG machine. Someone would then run into the room and fire a fake gun. Someone else would dance, a dog would bark, a color would be projected, and many other test situations were created. As the test subject was exposed to each situation, it caused their brain waves to form patterns on the recording instruments. Each situation was marked on the recording paper so the researchers would know what had transpired to create each pattern. "Dog barked here," as an example.

The next stage of the test was to have the subject sit and concentrate upon the situations described by the researchers. As an example, "I now want you to imagine yourself watching a woman dancing. See it in your mind, fantasize it, conceive it with as much imagination as possible . . . All right, I now want you to imagine a dog barking."

While the subject was concentrating upon these imagined situations, his brain waves were once again being recorded. The test results showed that identical patterns of up-and-down brain waves were created when the woman came into the room and danced as when the subjects imagined her dancing. The same was true with all the other situations with all the test subjects. *The brain waves were identical, so the computer part of the brain was obviously incapable of telling the real from the imagined.*

Another supportive series of tests was conducted by the University of Chicago. These and many similar tests show how our subconscious computer creates the reality for which it is programmed.

The subconscious can be fooled. It can be tricked. It can be programmed: you simply have to know how to become the programmer. This is one reason hypnosis works so effectively as a reprogramming technique.

It's also a very good reason to stop feeding your mind negativity. Instead, start reprogramming your mind with beneficial, life-affirming principles, and make your self-created reality a positive one.

1996

Integrating Your Fears

Your neurotic fears keep you from "wholeness" because they have not been integrated on a soul level. They are delusions manifesting as painful karma.

Your earthly purpose is to release the fear-based emotions that keep you earthbound on the endless wheel of reincarnation. The fears are only delusions, for as you learn to act with unconditional love and become aware of your spiritual center, the fears will cease to exist. Your earthly purpose, then, can be simplified down to just four words: *Cast away your delusions.*

I've made that statement in most of my seminars, but to be more accurate, I should say, *Your earthly purpose is to integrate the neurotic fears that keep you earthbound.* Examples of neurotic fears: prejudice, anger, selfishness, jealousy, hate, repression, envy, greed, possessiveness, guilt, and fear of intimacy, loss, abandonment, failure, success, loneliness, and power, to name a few.

To run from a bear in the woods, to avoid the wrong part of town at night, or to refrain from addictive drugs are fears based upon real dangers.

By contrast, neurotic fears are based on issues you have failed to integrate on a soul level. This keeps you from experiencing "wholeness." Example: If you are prejudiced toward East Indians, they somehow represent a subjective threat. When an East Indian couple moves next door, at first you are upset and reticent about contact. But there is no way to avoid occasional meetings as you come and go, water the lawn, pick up your mail. In time, you grow to like your new neighbors, and they become friends. The fear is integrated—replaced by a greater potential to enjoy life— and you are one step closer to wholeness.

Using the above example, it would also be accurate to say unconditional love resolved the fear: love let in what fear shut out. Unconditional love is the acceptance of others without expectations, judgment, or blame. Beneath all of our fears, we *are* unconditional love.

It follows that your current problems are rooted in one or more fear-based emotions. The fears go back to unintegrated issues, and they are your karma—the soul lessons you've reincarnated to learn.

Aliveness is the excitement you experience in doing what you do—the exhilaration, challenge, joy, stimulation, and pleasure that makes life worth living. According to the physicists, human beings are energy, and aliveness is essential to keep our energy at play. But when people don't experience aliveness, the subconsciousness mind draws upon neurotic fears to generate negative aliveness, which makes life interesting.

1997

The Cause of Being Overweight

If you can't lose weight, or if you quickly regain lost pounds, you're probably dealing with a karmic factor you need to know about. Something may have happened in the past (in this life or a past life) that is causing your subconscious mind to block your attempts to lose weight. In other words, your subconsciousness mind thinks you are being served by being overweight and overrides all efforts at self-discipline and dieting. The following are some real-life examples from my files.

Case 1

In an Atlanta seminar, a young, severely overweight woman explained that her doctor told her that her arches were breaking down because she was so heavy. She had tried every weight-loss program in the area, but as soon as she started to lose weight, she immediately would go on a binge and regain all the lost pounds.

As a demonstration, I regressed her back to the cause, and she found herself in revolutionary Europe. She was a pretty young teenager who lived a privileged life with her brother and parents. Then one day, the soldiers came to arrest the family, and it was the beginning of sexual abuse that ended with her death. She began to cry and said, "I was so pretty, and they killed me. If you want to be safe, you'll be ugly so they won't notice you."

Case 2

In a Palm Springs seminar, I conducted a "Back to the Cause" hypnotic regression and asked the participants to share what they experienced. A forty-year-old man stood up and said, "I explored the cause of being overweight, and saw myself at age five, sitting at the family dinner table back in Akron, Ohio. My mother was saying, 'Good boys, eat every bite,' over and over and over again. It was like a surreal nightmare."

Case 3

Somewhere between 5 and 10 percent of the people with a weight problem seem to have starved to death in a past life. That seems a little too obvious until you realize that throughout the world, millions of people a year still starve to death.

In a Los Angeles seminar, an overweight woman in her thirties relived a past life as a black woman in a primitive country. Drought had killed the animals, and her tribe starved to death. She explained, "I'm a very open, sharing person about everything, but food. I horde it, hide it, and overall feel desperate about it."

Case 4

In the late 1980s I regressed a woman named Eva. Her problem can be summarized as being hungry all her life but never being in a position to eat. Born in prewar Germany, her father withheld food to force her to learn to read and write faster than other children. She was thirteen at the end of World War II: "We were going through progressive starvation, until finally our food was cut off altogether. I had to beg from American soldiers or steal to stay alive."

As an adult, Eva found that if she ate more than 1000 calories a day, her weight ballooned. She said, "If all you can eat is 1000 calories, you are always hungry. So what I've been doing is eating normally for sixty days and gaining an immense amount of weight. Then I fast for thirty days and lose it again. Even this isn't working anymore. I think I'll have to eat for thirty days and fast for thirty days."

In regression, Eva was a ten-year-old named Mary. She was snowbound with thirty or forty others in the Donner party, a group of people who were trapped during a terrible winter in the mountains near Lake Tahoe in northern California. When directed forward to an important situation, she explained that her grandfather had just died, and it was mealtime. "Eva, and they don't want you to know that it's Grandfather. I just shouldn't be eating this." She began to tremble and cry.

This was the beginning of the terrible ordeal in which the survivors turned to cannibalism. Eva had been raised in Germany and had no conscious memory of ever having heard of the Donner party. Yet history supported all the details of her regressive experience. As one of the survivors, Mary lived a life of guilt, never even telling her husband of her experience. Even at death, after crossing over into spirit, she feared having to meet her grandfather again. In this life, Eva condemned herself to an entire lifetime of hunger as a way to deal with the guilt she was still feeling on a soul level.

If your weight problem relates to a past situation, finding the cause can help you to release the effect. Eva experienced false guilt karma, while the woman who felt she had to be ugly to be safe experienced false-fear karma. These kinds of karma can usually be released once the fear is fully understood. Balancing karma, and physical karma often take more effort to resolve.

No matter what the cause, you'll still need to follow an intelligent diet plan, but maybe your enlightened subconscious mind will no longer work against you.

1998

You Once Lived in Atlantis!

I've hypnotically regressed thousands of people back to Atlantis. It is rare that anyone is unable to recall at least one incarnation in that golden civilization.

In my early days of experimenting with past-life regression, I often directed groups back to a lifetime on the lost continent—even high-school classes in Scottsdale, Arizona. Many who participated had never heard of Atlantis or had no idea what the civilization was like. Yet most had a vivid experience, and invariably, they described a lifestyle and society I was already familiar with as the result of my own regression and those of my subjects.

Atlantis exists in our memory banks, or maybe within a "soul atom" that is part of our eternal identity.

1998

My husband wrote the following in January 1998 after his last trip with his then-wife to Australia. He knew their marriage was over and in some ways was writing this for himself. They continued to work together, not letting the public know they had split up until 2005.

A Zen story tells of two monks who met on the road. After their initial greetings, one monk asked the other, "What are you going to do tonight, my friend?"

The second monk replied, "I will meditate and pray in the temple. What are you going do do?"

"I'm going to spend a night of pleasure with the ladies," he answered.

The monks then went their own ways, and that night in the house of pleasure, the monk was quite distracted. All he could think about was his friend meditating and praying. But was the other monk at peace with himself? No, he continued to think about his friend enjoying an evening with the women.

Meditation: What decisions have you made that you're not fully accepting?

Afterthoughts: The decisions are *what is*, and it is your resistance to *what is* that causes your suffering. When you make a choice, accept it completely and surrender to all the experiences that go along with your decision. When the choice is made, stop evaluating and let go of your desires and expectations. Experience *what is*.

Once there was a man on a long journey who came to a river. He said to himself, "This side of the river is very difficult and dangerous to walk on, and the other side seems easier and safer, but how shall I get across?" After some deliberation, he built himself a raft out of branches and reeds and safely crossed the river. Then he thought, "This raft has been very useful to me in crossing the river, I will not abandon it to rot on the bank." So he hoisted the raft upon his back and proceeded on his journey, voluntarily assuming an unnecessary burden.

Even a good thing, when it becomes a burden, should be thrown away.

Meditation: What are you carrying on your back that is no longer necessary?

Consider releasing such things as negative friendships, old responsibilities, obligations, loyalties, and unhappy past, guilt, a philosophy, a belief, or material possessions. What are the first thoughts that jump into your mind? Consider the changes in your life that would lighten your load and allow you to proceed at a brisker, freer pace.

Afterthought: the idea is to let go of anything that is no longer useful and purposeful, and to do so without regrets or resentments. When you let go of what no longer serves you, you open the door to new adventures. But all too often we find security in the familiar and fear stops us from proceeding. Nietzsche framed the words, "Live dangerously," and hung them on his wall. He said he had done that as a reminder that his fear was tremendous. Hanging on the wall of my writing studio is a large reproduction of the words by Anaïs Nin: "Life shrinks or expands according to one's courage."

1998

Incompleteness

Incomplete cycles of action drain your energy and lower your self-esteem. Maybe it's time to act.

Those of you who have been with me in a seminar hopefully have clarity of intent. You have a vision for your life and you're taking steps to achieve that vision. The idea is to apply as much of your energy as possible to the direction you want to move, and refuse to waste it on activities that don't contribute.

What you may recognize is all the energy you waste on projects you don't complete—on incomplete cycles of action. The notion is that everything exists in three states: *idea*, *process*, and *completion*. Most of us have many things in our lives that are incomplete because, just short of the completion line—maybe 95 percent of the way to completion—is the finishing line. That's the place where we stop and say, "This will do." You've finished the project so that no one else will probably ever see its flaws, yet you haven't completed it to your own satisfaction.

Let's say one of your hobbies is building furniture. You decide upon the project of building a coffee table, so you go to a lumberyard and buy some beautiful rosewood. You take it to your workshop and go to work. You begin to carefully build an absolutely perfect table. Then you sand it until it's as smooth as gold and rub in the stain that sets off the grain. And then you apply about twenty coats of lacquer. You're really in love with this coffee table, and you've spent a lot of time on it.

It is nearly complete. Only the underside hasn't been varnished, and you're having a party this weekend, so you'd really like to move the table into the living room. You know you should go ahead and varnish the bottom, but you really don't have time, and who's ever going to look underneath the table anyway? You don't finish the underside.

So the weekend comes and all your friends attend the party. You have the table set up, and it looks fantastic. Every time someone walks into the room, they say, "What an incredible table. It's the most beautiful table I've ever seen."

Guess what's going on in your mind? "If only you could see the underside! I wish I'd finished it." That thought will haunt you every time someone comments on the table; every time you walk by the table; every time you see the table. And that really takes away your power. Because every time you look at the table and think about the underside not being varnished, a little bit of your energy goes—ZAP!—into the table. It's not completed to your satisfaction. It's just not finished. And what happens is, subconsciously, you may do something to break it, or maybe you hide it in a back room, or give it away just to get rid of the energy drain in your life.

Another example of an incomplete cycle of action—one that I relate to personally—is reading books. I love to read, and I spend a good portion of my time each day reading. Most of my friends know this and are readers themselves, so they're constantly recommending books for me to read. I'm also on the complimentary list of many publishers who send me new volumes they would like me to carry in my magazine. And our readers also send me books they are excited about.

Over the years, it has become increasingly difficult to keep my reading pile to a manageable size. The problem begins when I pick up a book to read, and after the first few pages, I'm saying, "I've already read ten books just like this one." Turning the pages is somewhat like nodding yourself to sleep, because you find yourself saying, "Uh huh, uh huh, yes, I know." At this point, I usually put the book away, thinking I might pick it up again when I run out of more interesting things to read. Of course, I never do, because there are an incredible number of interesting books to read. So in the past I had accumulated shelves and shelves of incomplete actions, and every time I looked at those rows of books, I felt a little overpowered, a little drained.

Often, I've given the books away, but bit by bit, I always manage to acquire new ones to take their place. I had finished the books—I'd read enough of them to know I didn't want to read more—yet I always wondered, "If I had read just a little farther, might I have learned something new?" I didn't feel complete.

Then, when I was doing research for my speed-reading tape, I figured out a way to complete all those damn books. Read the first few pages, skim every other page, or use the technique of reading the first sentence of each paragraph, then read the last page in each chapter, and read the last chapter of the book. Close the book and hold it in my hand for a few minutes to psychically absorb any information I missed, and put it back on the shelf—totally complete. End of energy drain.

In terms of personal power, it's infinitely more powerful to complete four things than to not finish ten. And it's a good idea to look at your life for areas where you have incomplete cycles of action. When you go back into your life and complete those things, you'll gain incredible personal power.

You may be wondering, "Does that mean I have to be a perfectionist about everything?" The answer is no, you only have to complete it to your satisfaction. And it's important to realize that sometimes completion is stopping a project—becoming clear that you no longer want to continue with it and stopping.

In seminar trainings, I tell participants not to take other people's opinions personally, good or bad, since they are coming from their viewpoint and really don't have anything to do with you. They would react the same way to anyone who represents to them what you represent. However, you must take your own opinions very seriously. That's where satisfaction of completion comes in. Let go of other people's expectations, and complete your projects to your own satisfaction.

Remember, self-esteem is generated by what you do in life, and what you think about what you do in life. And high self-esteem is critical to your happiness.

2003

The World as a Teaching Device

Some mystics call the world a "teaching device." In other words, your karma put you in this place, at this time, with these people, living in a world that appears to be spinning out of control, just to give you an opportunity to learn. How you respond to your tests will dictate whether or not you pass the class.

If you want an A in "Earth Life" class, the best response is to be *in* the world but not *of* it.

Easier said than done when confronted with personal problems, terrorist threats, and the potential of war. Physical escape might be a consideration if there were somewhere to go. But your personal problems will follow you anywhere. Terrorists even strike in remote South Sea islands. Nuclear fallout is global.

Mind is your only refuge—to go within the calm center of the cyclone. Whenever you're upset, stressed, or suffering, your expectations are in conflict with *what is*. You think things could or should be different than they are. You expect your mate to be loyal and loving, but that's not *what is*. So you get upset. You expect your lifestyle to remain stable, but because of the economic downturn, that's not *what is*. So you worry and fear. You want terrorists to go away, but that's not *what is*. So you manifest stress.

The way you view things creates the cyclone.

And the way you view things can keep you in the calm center of the cyclone.

To quell the chaos, cease to resist *what is*. Accept that you cannot control other people or worldly events. And let go of the past and future. The past no longer exists, and the future is yet to come. You exist in the eternal now. And NOW . . . right NOW, what is lacking? Obviously you're still here . . . surviving. Your life is not in danger right NOW. Dwelling on the past creates suffering. Worrying about the future creates suffering. Catch yourself and cancel the past/future mind-programming by saying, "I'm living right NOW."

According to Zen, if you're wondering where you're karmically supposed to be right NOW, look down at your feet.

Stop looking for meaning in the chaos. Even when you think you've found meaning, today's interpretation probably won't relate tomorrow. You don't really need to know why. You simply need to accept *what is* and stop trying to control outcomes. Trying to manipulate a situation to be the way you want it to be seldom works over the long run. However, being loving and compassionate often alters an outcome in lasting ways.

Detached mind is very freeing. Say yes to life, and allow the negativity to flow through you without affecting you. Recognize the importance of this goal. You can't change what you don't recognize. It does take time and attention, but you can do it. And it will be worth it.

2004

A Path with Heart

"Always follow your heart, it knows the way," is a hand-lettered sign on the copy board by my computer.

Eastern wisdom says, "Follow the path with a heart."

You could interpret this "heart wisdom" to mean following a path that resonates with who you are, what you want to be, where you find joy, and who you want to be with.

Or you can look at the wisdom from a higher perspective, which perceives your spiritual heart to be the center of your soul. This spiritual heart is your connection to God, the Tao, the Universe, the All That Is.

According to the mystics, if you can move your consciousness from your head to your heart, you will transcend all problems. Freedom from the self will be found by following this heart-centered path through life.

The path is a state of consciousness—a mindset allowing you to be in the world but not of it. There are five steps to put you on the path.

1. **Accept self-responsibility.** If you accept karma, you accept that you and you alone are responsible for your experiences. There is no one to blame. You needed each unpleasant (or downright painful) experience in your past to teach yourself what you came here to learn. What were the lessons? *You don't want to miss the lessons.* Accept others without judgment, blame, expectations, or attempting to control.

2. **Accept *what is*.** When you recognize *what is*, you stop wasting mental or physical energy attempting to change what cannot be changed. I am not advising you to passively accept life. What you have the potential to change, go ahead and change. But recognize the things you can do nothing about and stop wasting your time complaining about them. Gravity exists; that's *what is*. Your mate is quiet and stubborn; that's *what is*. Greedy corporations exist; that's *what is*.

3. **Develop detached mind.** When your state of mind fluctuates only from positive to neutral as outside conditions change, you have learned detachment. Accept self-responsibility, accept *what is*, and monitor reactions that are not in keeping with the above. Detached mind will result.

4. **Monitor viewpoint.** The way you experience life results from the way you choose to view what happens to you. Your viewpoint is the deciding factor in whether you experience a situation positively or negatively.

5. **Act with compassion.** Compassion is passion transformed—a desirelessness state of mind from which you give mercy or supply aid with no expectation of acknowledgment.

About the Authors

Roberta Sutphen was married to and worked alongside her beloved husband, Dick Sutphen, for over a decade before he passed away his sleep on the morning of September 1, 2020. Although he is in Spirit, he is still very much involved in Roberta's life and looked over her shoulder as she put this book together.

Dick Sutphen spent over fifty years researching human-potential and psychic abilities. He was known as "America's Leading Past-Life Therapist" by the Body Mind Spirit Festivals in England and Australia. As a specialist in Past-Life Regression and Spirit-Contact Therapy®, he had a private hypnotherapy practice, and was the first to mass-produce audio and video programs.

Dick created and conducted Master of Life, Bushido, and other Psychic and Reincarnation Seminars world-wide and developed innovative group hypnosis exploration techniques that are now being used internationally. Over a half million people have attended one of Dick's seminars.

As a professional hypnotherapist, he was well known for his hypnotist trainings and has received numerous awards.

Between 1976 and 2012, Dick wrote, produced, and recorded over 900 audio and video programs including hypnosis, meditations, sleep programming, and audio books.

Dick was an amazing man who gave us so much wisdom over a fifty-year career.

This book is for all of Dick's students, seminar participants, and anyone in the hypnosis field who want to experience the words of a Master.

CPSIA information can be obtained
at www.ICGtesting.com
Printed in the USA
JSHW011031030523
41198JS00005B/8